Tim

Happy Browsing
Safe Motoring
Happy CRImBo

With Much Love
Anne + John
1988

MOTO GUZZI TWINS

OSPREY
COLLECTOR'S
LIBRARY

MOTO GUZZI TWINS

All V-twins, 350 through 1000 cc, plus parallel twins— 1964 onwards

Mick Walker

First published in 1986 by Osprey Publishing Limited
27A Floral Street, London WC2E 9DP
Member company of the George Philip Group
Reprinted spring 1988

British Library Cataloguing in Publication Data

Walker, Mick
    Moto Guzzi twins: V-twins, 350 through 1000 cc,
    plus parallel twins—1964 onwards.
    —(Osprey collector's library)
    1. Moto Guzzi motorcycle—History
    I. Title
    629.2'275   TL448.M66
ISBN 0-85045-650-9

Associates Andrew Kemp and Amedeo
Castellani

Filmset and printed in England by
BAS Printers Limited, Over Wallop, Hampshire

Contents

Foreword by Roy Armstrong

Winner of the prestigious British Avon Production series
in the unlimited class was Roy Armstrong (52) on his (Mk
I) Le Mans; the year is 1977. Other riders in the frame are
Phil Mellor (26) and Richard Stevens (14), both Yamaha
mounted

After many years of regular day-to-day motorcycling, I still enjoyed riding, but not actually owning my various bikes. Then came the 'Italian' way, and immediately appearance, style *and* functional design were fused into a single motorcycle.

My initial Guzzi involvement came about by working on early V-twin models such as the 850T. Then came 1975, and the debut of the 850 Le Mans at the autumn shows—this was the one. It was love at first sight and both my brother and I purchased machines. I soon found that I wanted to go racing with the Italian sportster. This was against all the advice from the pundits—'shaft drive bikes don't handle, a shaft drive absorbs too much power, and pushrod engines are not suitable for racing'. The success I had racing my Guzzi proved the pundits wrong in the extreme. . . .

To begin racing the Le Mans, the modifications I made amounted to fitting a racing camshaft and cleaning up the inlet ports—that's all. The race results soon started to come, but more speed was needed, so in July 1977 stronger valve springs and special 88 mm pistons were obtained from Italy. With these fitted the Le Mans suddenly became the machine to try and beat; with the greater performance available the handling could now be exploited to the full. Another aspect of racing the Le Mans was its excellent level of reliability. This is clearly shown by the fact that both my brother Ian's bike and my own ran the whole 1977 racing season, and made excursions to Wales and the Lake District and several other journeys, with only one failure between the bikes. This was when I over-revved mine in the heat of racing with the result that the valves kissed the pistons at 10,000 rpm. Even after such treatment the engine still remained quiet and reliable.

The V-twin Guzzi has become a classic design, but unlike many other classics, which often achieve fame only after becoming extinct, it is also a commercial success.

The Moto Guzzi company has had 65 years as a manufacturer, and been through a World War, producing efficient, reliable and, and at the same time, exciting motorcycles. Whenever Guzzi display a new model, it is innovative, with the result that the motorcycling world never fails to take notice. It is this special 'knack' which gives Guzzi its unique place in the hearts of many enthusiasts around the world.

It has been a privilege and a pleasure to have been associated with the winged eagle over many years, first as a mechanic and part-time racer, and now through the Moto Guzzi agency, Italsport, that I run in Manchester.

I am sure you will find this book both informative and interesting, giving as it does a detailed insight into the Guzzi Twins and their achievements over the years.

Roy Armstrong
Winner Avon British Production Bike
Championship on a Guzzi Le Mans 1977

Manchester, October 1985

Acknowledgements

The author (right) looks pensive, whilst ex-British road racing champion Dave Croxford on a California looks keen. February 1976 at the opening of the massive 22,000 sq ft showroom complex of Mick Walker Motorcycles in Norwich Road, Wisbech

This book came about as a direct result of my two previous titles in the Osprey Collector's Series, DUCATI SINGLES and DUCATI TWINS. Moto Guzzi, like Ducati, has played an important role in my life for a good many years, first as a motorcyle I admired in my youth and then as one I worked on, so once again much of my experience is first hand. After becoming the British spares importer for the marque in May 1975, the following years saw my enthusiasm for, and knowledge of, this unique range of motorcycles grow even stronger.

What has always impressed me most about the Guzzi V-twin, which I feature particularly, is the toughness of the engine combined with the ease with which maintenance work can be carried out. I well recall the first ever Guzzi V-twin which my company, Mick Walker Motorcycles, purchased early in 1975. An 850T, this was stripped for spares in our showroom, down to almost the last nut and bolt, using only the toolkit provided with the machine!

As with previous titles, I have found that my great number of friends within the motorcycling world have played an important role in this latest work: some with words of wisdom and yet others with vital snippets of priceless information.

Two people in particular who gave much valuable time and assistance were Amedeo Castellani and Vincent Marcello: thank you both. I also received help from Moto Guzzi, via their export sales manager and old friend, Sig. 'Joe' Ermilini, and also through the current British importer,

Keith Davies of Three Cross Motorcycles.

Many Guzzi owners around the world provided their own personal experiences, and as usual I found in particular that those who have raced the twins were able to share their track exploits so that I could record a host of interesting facts.

A special thank you to my pal from Ludlow, Doug Jackson, who once again came up trumps with many superb pictures from his collection, and who also offered real encouragement when the going got tough. Thanks also to Peter Maskell of EMAP, who, through Brian Wooley, provided many important photographs from the *Motor Cycle Weekly* archives and also to the following craftsmen (in alphabetical order): Ian Brambley, Tony Charnock, J. Clayton, Bruce Cox, D. Dixon, Calbifoto, Jan Heese, E. Leverkus, S. Mallinson, D. Nash, P. Norden, Tim Parker, Carlo Perelli, R. Pontiroli Gobbi, G. Pini, Rod Sloane, Richard Stevens, Don Upshaw, Richard Walker, David Burgess Wise and M. Woollett. Thank you all.

My choice for the foreword, Roy Armstrong, typifies the real spirit of the racing privateer. Against the odds, he won one of the most prestigious events ever staged for sports machines, the Avon Production Series, aboard his Le Mans.

Finally, I wish to thank as usual the Osprey Publishing team, Tim Parker, Helen John and Joanne Stone and not least Andrew Kemp, for their unstinting assistance with this title, which sets out to record the full story of the Guzzi twins.

Mick Walker
Wisbech, Cambridgeshire
October 1985

1 The Mandello eagle

Mandello del Lario is hardly more than a large village, situated on the eastern shores of Lake Como, in the extreme north of Italy, a few kilometres north of the town of Lecco. But since the birth of the Moto Guzzi factory just after the First World War, it has become famous the world over as the home of a motorcycling legend.

This legend is the result of the men and the machinery who have combined to produce a unique cocktail of motorcycling history down the years. Moto Guzzi's 'secret' has been their ability to carve a niche which the company's products have consistently filled with up-market, soundly-engineered motorcycles, retaining a quality and sporting character which the opposition have always found difficult to match. And for the greater part of their history, enthusiasm for the commercial product was fuelled by Guzzi's all-conquering track exploits.

Squadron life in the Italian Air Service of 1918 may seem a strange background in which to talk about plans for building a new motorcycle, but this is exactly where the now-famous Guzzi marque was born. Two pilots, Giorgio Parodi and Giovanni Ravelli, both had the services of a talented young mechanic/driver named Carlo Guzzi. Guzzi had one great passion—to design his own motorcycle—which was of particular interest to Ravelli, already a motorcycle enthusiast and prewar race winner, who soon formed the opinion that Carlo Guzzi's ideas had much to recommend them. Even though the war-torn Italy of 1918 hardly seemed the time or the place to do much about it, for a bitterly-contested air war had been fought with the neighbouring Austro-Hungary for three long years, the young airmen laid plans for the future.

Sadly, Ravelli was doomed never to see Guzzi's handiwork come to fruition, losing his life while flying, shortly after the end of the war in September 1918. But both Giorgio Parodi and Carlo Guzzi survived the conflict, and the pair decided to press on with the wartime dream of their own brand of motorcycle.

Their first main problem was finance, but although Guzzi himself had little means, luckily Parodi was from a wealthy family. His father, Emanuele, was a rich shipping line owner from Genoa, and on 3 January, 1919, Parodi Senior sent a three-page letter (the original of which can still be seen in the Guzzi museum) confirming that he would help fund the construction of the

first prototype to the tune of 1500 to 2000 lire. His price was the right to assume control of the fledgling enterprise, which was accepted by all the participants in the project, simply because it gave a level of stability and professional business leadership to a set-up which might otherwise have been engulfed by amateur enthusiasm.

With finance, and the design drawn up in detail, it was time to set about transforming the idea into a reality in metal. The first prototype was given the name G.P., (for Guzzi-Parodi), but by the time the magazine *Motociclismo* announced the new marque publicly for the first

The original G & P (Guzzi & Parodi) horizontal 500 cc single, the forerunner of over half a century's use by Guzzi of the basic design; the year is 1920

time on 15 December 1920, the name had been changed to the familiar Moto Guzzi. Not only this, but the fledgling firm had adopted a new trademark, of an eagle with its wings spread in flight. The emblem, proudly borne by Guzzi motorcycles to this day, was selected by Guzzi and Parodi to record the memories of their dead comrade Giovanni Ravelli, and the air service in which they had all served.

For its day, the prototype was a revolutionary design. Its 498·4 cc single cylinder engine was laid horizontally and had an overhead cam driven by shaft and bevel gears. Perhaps even more interesting was the four-valve head layout, and the engine's oversquare (short-stroke) dimensions with its 88 × 82 mm bore and stroke.

The first production models closely followed the original scheme but the overhead cam was changed to overhead valve operation, and the machine had a more conventional two-valve cylinder head. The 1921 production model was named the Tipo Normale (standard model) and produced 8 bhp at 3200 rpm, driving the rear wheel through a three-speed gearbox and a chain on the right-hand side of the machine.

The new company's ten employees produced 17 motorcycles in that first year, but the design, with its massive outside flywheel, semi-unit construction gearbox, and magneto ignition mounted centrally above the engine/gearbox was to

1924 4-valve 500 racer ridden by European champion Guido Mentasti ; note the massive 'bacon slicer' outside flywheel

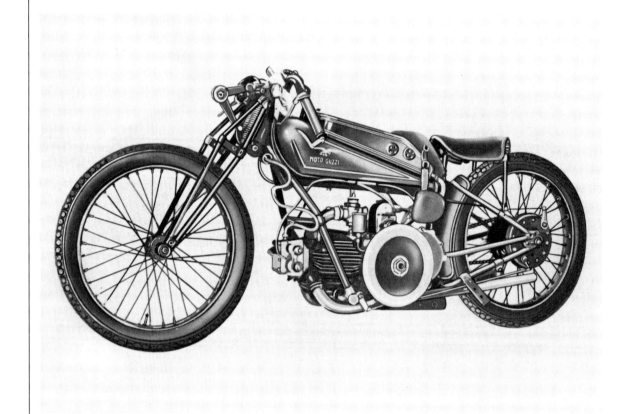

remain in production, albeit updated from time to time, until as late as 1976—still retaining its original 88 × 82 mm engine dimensions.

Over the years, many variations of the classic format appeared, including the Tipo GP, Tipo Sport, GT and GT16, Tipo Sport 14 and 15, V, GTV, GTW, GTC, S, GTS, the Condor clubman's racer, the Dondolino (strictly, a little rocking chair), clubman's racer, Astore (goshawk)—and finally, perhaps the best-known of all—the Falcone.

The original Falcone was produced from 1950 until 1967, with a revised version, the Nuova Falcone, being made from 1970 until 1976. It was

also made in police and military forms, as indeed were several of the other models.

Apart from this wide range of '500s', the flat single layout was also produced in other capacities. The first was the 174 cc P175 of 1932, followed a derivative of 238 cc, the P250. Production of both of these models ceased with Italy's entry into WW2 on 10 June 1940. But in any case, an improved 250, the Airone (heron) had appeared in 1939, and this model remained in production until as late as 1957. The Airone, with its 247 cc engine, was available in touring or sports guise, and was an extremely popular model in the boom days of postwar Italy.

Right from the start, Moto Guzzi had realized that there was no better publicity than participation in racing. So in 1921, to launch the first prod-

Luxury three-cylinder Guzzi pictured during 1933 at a show, probably in Milan

ucts, the factory entered Aldo Finzi and Gino Cavedini for the Milano-Napoli long-distance race on a pair of 500 Guzzis. Both completed the event to become the first 'works' Guzzi riders of a new era which was eventually to see the Mandello del Lario factory reach the very pinnacle of the sport. Finzi and Cavendini took 20th and 22nd placings, and with their efforts proved the reliability of the new bikes—a feature that was to play such an important part in the success of future racing Guzzis.

Moto Guzzi's confidence was shown to be well-founded just over a month later, when Finzi's brother Gino won the arduous Targa Florio in Sicily, then open to both cars and motorcycles. And in the next year, 1922, Guzzi gained still more racing successes again using machines based on the standard production models.

But racing needs soon led to the re-adoption of the very first prototype's single overhead cam and four-valve head. The new machine had its debut at the local Circuito del Lario—the Italian equivalent of the Isle of Man TT, with 50 kilometres of public roads near the factory's base. In a stunning debut, the new ohc Guzzi with Guido Mentasi aboard swept to an unexpected victory against the best riders of the day.

International recognition came the following year, when Mentasi triumphed in the European Championship race at Monza, and then again

246·8 cc single, based on the larger Guzzi single, won the Lightweight TT in the IoM in 1935, the first TT win by a foreign make since the American firm, Indian, took the Senior in 1911. Rider was Irishman Stanley Woods

250cc. T.T.-1935 (Corsa)

two weeks later, when Mario Ghersi capped this by winning the German Grand Prix. By now, Moto Guzzi was well and truly on its way, with the factory selling everything that it could make, and clear signals indicating that it was set to become one of the biggest in Italy.

Assisted by his elder brother, Giuseppe, Carlo Guzzi had also designed a $\frac{1}{4}$ litre racer. Unlike its larger counterpart, this had square dimensions at 68 × 68 mm, giving a capacity of 246·8 cc. Ultimately this gave some 15 bhp at 6000 rpm, and the new bike, which made its debut in 1926, was to feature prominently in Guzzi's first appearance in the Isle of Man TT that year.

The results were not quite what Guzzi had hoped, and it was an unfortunately controversial introduction to the Island. For although works entrant Pietro Ghersi finished second in the light-weight race, he was disqualified on a trivial technical rule. Ghersi had substituted another type of spark plug for the one on his original race entry form! At the time, it was argued by the race officials that Ghersi had been warned before the race started that he was liable to suffer disqualification for infringing the rule book, but he in turn had argued that as a 'visitor', he should receive special concessions. Ghersi was no doubt to regret the spark plug incident, as he not only finished in second spot, but recorded the fastest lap into the bargain.

Nine years later, in 1935, Guzzi at least, if not Ghersi, were to have their revenge when Irish-man Stanley Woods won the Lightweight TT for the marque. Not only did he take the race, but also the class lap record, despite poor visibility on the mountain section. And for the factory, it was not only the first TT win by a foreign make since the American firm, Indian, took the Senior in 1911, but it was also the first TT win by a spring-framed machine.

Racing was what ushered in the first Guzzi twin, the main theme of this book. The Bicilindrica (twin cylinder) 120 degree 494·8 cc V-twin made its first appearance in 1933 and was still

Horizontal four-cylinder 500 supercharged racing engine of 1930. Although its frame would date the bike, the engine still looks up-to-date—a fitting compliment to its talented designer Carlo Guzzi

being raced as late as 1951, 18 years on. Guzzi's first twin cylinder design was a real tour de force. As the observant reader will have noticed, its dimensions show that it was a doubling-up of the successful earlier 250 cc racer, so it is all the more significant that a couple of days after Stanley Woods' 250 win, Guzzi were victorious in the most important and prestigious race of the era—the blue riband Senior TT. Woods also made history by becoming the first man to win both the 250 and 500 TT races in the same year.

More records were set two years later when Omobono Tenni became the first Italian to win a TT by finishing ahead of the field in the 1937 Lightweight race after a superbly professional ride, still remembered by those who witnessed it as one of the most terrific performances in the annals of pre-war racing on the famous Mountain circuit.

Less successful, but still a highly interesting Guzzi racer of pre-war days was the horizontal

four-cylinder 500 of 1930. Although its frame technology was clearly of the period, the engine design still looks up-to-date—a fitting compliment to its talented creator. With full unit construction and supercharging, it was a long-stroke at 52 × 60 mm bore and stroke, giving a capacity of 492·2 cc.

Like so many other things, the factory's smooth running was rudely interrupted between 1940 and 1945, when Italy was embroiled in the world-wide hostilities. Leading up to this time, and for most of World War 2, Guzzi were involved in supplying the Italian military authorities with a series of motorcycles expressly for military use, but fortunately, Guzzi's lake-side location in mountainous country protected it during the heavy Allied bombing of northern

The first version of the 120 degree 494·8 cc V-twin made its first appearance in 1933

Italy from 1943 until the end of the war. As a result, unlike many other plants, they were in a position to resume production of civilian motorcycles and recommence their race effort almost at once when the war ended.

One exciting project which appeared in 1940, but had to be laid aside, was a three-cylinder 491·8 cc racer producing 65 bhp at 8000 rpm. But when the factory started again in 1946, the race effort had to concentrate on well-tried hardware, almost entirely the traditional singles, even though there was still the 120-degree V-twin, now modernized and producing more power.

1937 shot of the V-twin racer, at a Grand Prix on the Continent

The twin soon sported leading link forks, together with massive full-width drum brakes (double-sided twin-leading shoe at the front). The new forks were designed by Antonio Micucci and first appeared on the V-twin in 1949. They were to become a hallmark of the factory racers throughout the 1950s.

The Isle of Man TT remained an important part of Guzzi's racing plans. The factory's policy was rewarded by them gaining several postwar TT victories. Stanley Woods' protégé Manliff Barrington won the Lightweight event in 1947, Maurice Cann repeated the performance in 1948, Barrington won again in 1949, Tommy Woods did it in 1951, while Fergus Anderson won in 1952 and again in 1953. These victories were followed by Bill Lomas and Ken Kavanagh who became Junior TT winners in 1955 and 1956 respectively.

Only a year later, the long connection with road racing came to an end, when Guzzi joined Gilera and FB Mondial in withdrawing from the sport. For many, this was to mark the end of an era, viewed now as the golden days of the European racing effort. By then, Guzzi had scored more than 3000 international racing victories throughout the world, and no fewer than eight world championships—Bruno Ruffo, 1949 and 1951 250 cc; Enrico Lorenzetti, 1952 250 cc; Fergus Anderson, 1953 and 1954 350 cc; Bill

Left **An exciting project which appeared in 1940, but which had to be laid aside at the onset of war, was this blown three-cylinder 500 racer, which produced 65 bhp @ 8000 rpm**

Below left **Two-fifty twin cylinder racer of 1947, one of the first Guzzis to employ telescopic front forks**

Beautiful period shot of Guzzi factory mechanics working on a 500 V-twin racer during the 1949 IoM TT

Lomas, 1955 and 1956 350 cc; and finally, Keith Campbell, 1957 350 cc.

Hidden amongst these facts and figures are many interesting racing machines, including the 250 twin-cylinder of 1947–48, the in-line, shaft-drive, four-cylinder of 1952–54, and a design that to this day is held up as the greatest racing motorcycle of all time, the awesome V8 500.

Of all the designs recorded above, the one that achieved the most was a direct descendant of the very first Guzzi—the horizontal 350 single which scored five successive world championships, beating the best four-cylinder designs that MV Agusta and Gilera could field against it.

Following the Second World War, Moto Guzzi had reinforced its position as the largest of all Italy's motorcycle manufacturers, with a range that included several popular models, among which the Airone and Falcone were top sellers. Soon, these were joined by new designs, including the 65 cc Motoleggera (lightweight motor-

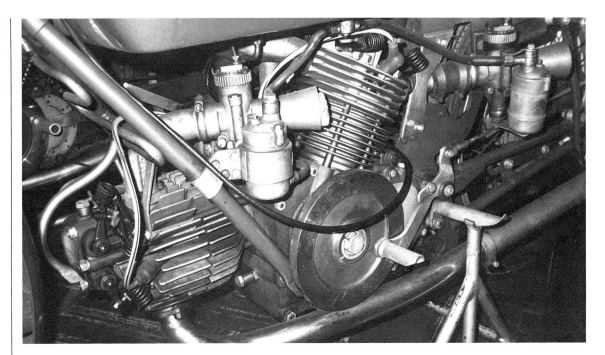

Left **Engine close-up shot of the V-twin showing Dell'Orto carburettors, exposed hairpin valve springs and wide angle of the cylinders to advantage. This actual machine is now housed in the Guzzi Museum at Mandello**

Below left **Paddock shot taken at the German Grand Prix of 1951, in the foreground (30) is a five-hundred V-twin**

cycle) and Cardellino (goldfinch) two-strokes, and the Galletto (rooster), which was a successful cross between a scooter and a conventional motorcycle, with first a capacity of 160 cc, later upped to 192 cc—both engines being horizontal ohv, with three and four-speed gearboxes respectively. In its various forms, the Galletto had a production life span of 16 years from 1950 to 1966.

Similarly long-lived was the 98 cc rotary valve two-stroke Zigolo (bunting). The sporting Lodola (hobby) introduced in 1956 was another single, but this was a four-stroke with a vertical cylinder and chain-driven overhead cam. Up to 1958, the Lodola had a capacity of 174 cc, but for 1959, this was increased to 235 cc but 'reduced' to ohv. Besides its standard and sportster versions, it was a successful entrant in the ISDT for Italian team riders in 175, 235 and a special version of 247 cc.

Another four-stroke single produced in more

Works rider Fergus Anderson and the 500 cc in-line four cylinder racer, Italian Grand Prix 1953

Engines on display in the Guzzi Museum in 1984; the 250 4-valve single of 1932 and the 1951 in-line 500 four

Below Carcano's masterpiece, the legendary V8 five hundred Grand Prix racer, with hand beaten alloy dustbin fairing and seat

than one size was the Stornello (starling). This was available from 1960 to 1968 as a 125 only, thereafter joined by a 160 cc version. This was also produced in a Six-Days trial form, but only in the smaller capacity class.

The Dingo and the Trotter were both small-capacity two-strokes. The Dingo was available from 1973 through to 1976. It had a 48·9 cc engine and was built in just about every conceivable version from the Turismo commuter moped, right through to the Dingo Super Sport and Cross models for the young enthusiast. The Trotter was a 40·8 cc two-speed commuter model, looking very much like a Guzzi-made Vespa Ciao.

Another important facet of Guzzi production was the Motocarri series. These were essentially a cross between a motorcycle (the front half), and a lightweight truck (the back half). The first version, the Tipo 107, was first offered for sale in 1928, powered by the familiar 498·4 cc horizontal single. Amazingly, the Motocarri 500 cc was listed from then until 1980 (except for the war years), making it Guzzi's longest-running model ever. In that time, the basic concept was unchanged, and after 52 years the final model could be seen to have much in common with the first.

The reason for the machine's exceptionally long life span was the practical use to which the three-wheel vehicle could be put. At minimum running cost, it could cope with almost every urban task from goods delivery to sewage collection, plus everything in between.

The same design was made in other engine sizes as the 192 cc Galletto-powered Motocarri Ercolino (Little Hercules) 1956–70 and the short-lived 110 Zigolo-based Motocarri Alce (1962–63).

There were also moped-based three-wheelers called Ciclocarros. The first was the Ciclocarro Dingotre (dingo?) (1965–68), followed by the Ciclocarro Furghino (small van) (1968–71). And several interesting Motocarri prototypes were built including a 238 cc flat single in 1934 and finally a flat-twin diesel-powered three-wheeler in 1960.

But it was an even less obvious source which ultimately produced the engine configuration which forms the main content of this book—the 90 degree ohv V-twin. For this was spawned by a line of military vehicles.

It began with the Mototriciclo 32, which used the standard 498·4 cc horizontal single engine. The '32' had the front section of a 1933 Sport 15 mated to a twin wheel chassis like that on the civilian Motocarri. But in military use, the Guzzi three-wheeler did not achieve the level of success its civilian counterpart had managed and only remained in production until 1936.

Just prior to the war, and during its course, Guzzi built a three-wheel armoured machine-gun carrier, and an experimental miniature tank which was designed to operate on steep hillsides by extending one track below the other. And the factory even built a military truck with two wheels at the front and one at the rear, powered by a rear-mounted 500 cc flat-single.

More conventional military offerings then included the GT, and Alce, followed postwar by the Superalce and Falcone as described in chapter 12. But it was in 1960 that a strange new military vehicle called the 3 × 3 first appeared.

This was the brainchild of General Garbari, and the engine which was to play such an important part in Moto Guzzi's future was designed specially for it by none other than the gifted designer who had, almost at the drop of a hat, produced the classic 1950s Guzzi racers—Ing. Giulio Cesare Carcano. According to Mario Colombo in his book, the V7 engine originally started life as a souped-up version for the Fiat Topolino. First a 500, then a 650 cc engine was made which fitted perfectly to the Fiat's transmission. The larger version developed some 34 hp and was capable of propelling the vehicle to 140 km/h. A lack of agreement with Fiat finally killed the project but the basic engine design was then used in the 3 × 3 albeit in detuned form.

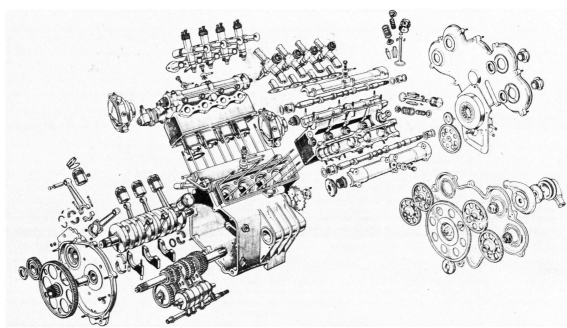

Above **This bizarre vehicle, the military 3 × 3 tractor, used a 90 degree V-twin engine of 754 cc, which was later to spawn the classic range of Guzzi V-twin motorcycles**

Left above **Engine of the V8, illustrating how close together the eight carburettors were, a real shoehorn job**

Left below **Exploded view, exposing perhaps the most famous road racing engine of all time**

The 3 × 3 itself must surely go down in history as one of the most bizarre-looking wheeled contraptions of all time. During the late 1950s, the Italian Defence Ministry in Rome first conceived the requirement for a go-anywhere, lightweight tractor to operate under almost any condition, over any terrain including deep sand or snow. The final result of this complex specification was a three-wheel vehicle which plainly owed much to the Guzzi Motocarri principle.

But the 3 × 3 was equipped for almost everything—and could even climb almost vertical surfaces! The driver sat out in the open, and unlike the normal Motocarri, the 3 × 3 had a steering wheel and car-type steering column. Behind him was a 53-litre fuel tank and spare wheel. The single front and twin rear wheels all carried heavy-duty 6·00 × 15 in. tyres, and for heavy going, the rear wheels could also be fitted with tracks after lowering retractable bogey wheels.

But it was the engine layout which created so much of interest and importance for the future. It was a 90 degree V-twin ohv of 754 cc with a bore and stroke of 80 × 75 mm. The power was only 20 bhp at 4000 rpm, but with massive torque generation which made it ideal for its

intended role. The compression ratio was equally low at 6·5 : 1. At the rear of the engine was a single plate dry clutch, and behind this was a six-speed gearbox which drove the rear wheels by Cardan shaft.

Although only produced in limited quantities between 1960 and 1963, the extraordinary 3 × 3's power unit and drive train had sown important seeds for a new and exciting era for Moto Guzzi enthusiasts the world over. For from this unlikely source was to be born a range of motorcycles which would become as well-loved as the classic horizontal singles—the V-twins which this book is all about.

The Guzzi 3 × 3 was equipped for almost everything—it could even climb almost vertical surfaces as this picture proves

2 | V7—touring beginnings

The origins of the large-capacity V-twin Guzzi motorcycles came almost entirely from the firm's involvement with Italy's military and civil authorities. The V-twin power unit itself started life as the engine for the extraordinary light-weight three-wheeler which Moto Guzzi designed for the army, and the idea of using this as the basis of a roadster motorcycle was greatly assisted in its infancy by the Italian government's need for a suitable replacement for its ageing Guzzi flat-single Falcone models, used in both military and police work.

The first prototype of what was ultimately to emerge as the V7 was begun in 1964. Early the next year, the original pre-production models went up for government official inspection, and the full story of what happened to them is told in chapter 12. But even before the official tests had begun, Guzzi knew that the machine was destined to be a success in the wider field of everyday riding, and the first civilian prototype appeared in public for the first time soon after, in December 1965 at the 39th International Milan Show. It was immediately hailed as the star exhibit and leading journalist of the time, Carlo Perelli, saw the new 700 Guzzi V-twin as 'leading Italy in fighting for home and export markets'.

The background to this remark was the public awareness of a serious sales crisis, with the Italian motorcycle industry attempting to stem a drop of some 30 per cent since the previous year—which had itself seen a steady decline. But unlike most of the British industry of the period, which

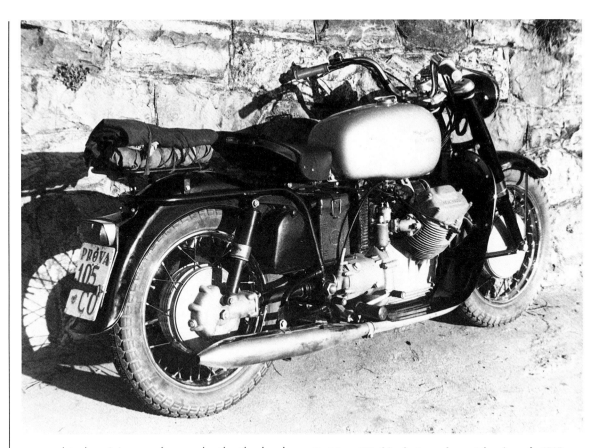

Prototype V7 ; this photograph was taken in early 1965, when the machine was being evaluated by the Italian police and military authorities

seemed to be giving up despondently, the leading Italian factories were not prepared to take this lying down. Instead, they had made a strong bid to revive interest in a pastime that only short years before had enjoyed the eager support of more than two million of their fellow countrymen. So the 1965 Milan Show saw a whole crop of exciting new models launched by many of the most famous names in the Italian motorcycle industry, including MV, Benelli, Morini, Laverda, Gilera and Ducati—but the new Guzzi heavyweight stole their thunder in no uncertain terms.

The V7, a big bike by any standards, was also the biggest and fastest roadster ever to have rolled off the famous production line at Mandello del Lario. But like many a famous machine before it, it owed much to the brilliance of the gifted engineer behind the greatest Guzzis, Ing. Giulio Cesare Carcano. Less than a decade before, his fertile brain had brought the world what is possibly the most famous racing motorcycle of all time, the legendary 498 cc Grand Prix Moto Guzzi V8. The tremendous speed and awesome technical specifications of this masterpiece are still held in awe by racing enthusiasts even today. During the 1957 Belgian Grand Prix, the fabulous water-cooled, dustbin-faired V8 had been timed at over 178 mph, and, without doubt, if Guzzi (along with Gilera and FB Mondial) had not pulled

Out on an Italian mountain road, a factory tester has pulled off (for a rest?); spring 1965

out of racing at the end of the year, Carcano's masterpiece would have ruled the world for a good many years, and Guzzi, not MV, would have taken the victor's rostrum in the supreme road racing championship — the 500 cc class.

As it was, at least one result of the decision to pull out of racing was that Moto Guzzi lost a valuable amount of publicity, and this was ultimately to hasten the marque's decline in the early 1960s. But now it looked as if the V7 project had at last produced the sort of exciting machine for which Guzzi had been famous, and it had cer-

tainly restored their name to enthusiasts' lips everywhere.

Unlike Guzzi's racing exotica, the original V7's engine was obviously designed with priority given to simplicity and ease of maintenance. In many ways, in fact, for a motorcycle design it was surprisingly 'agricultural', especially when compared with some of the more exotic creations of the Superbike era, into which its long life was to take it. The V7 name was drawn from the engine's transverse 90 degree V-twin layout, and its original capacity of 703·717 cc. This ohv power unit had over-square dimensions with bore and stroke of 80 × 70 mm, and on a compression ratio of 9:1, it gave 50 bhp at a leisurely (by later standards) 6000 rpm.

The engine layout gave superb accessibility,

and its simplicity and relatively 'soft' stage of tune made for a long, maintenance-free life. These characteristics were to prove the design's strongest and most appealing assets over the years. There were, however, one or two features which seemed at odds with the designer's priorities as evidenced elsewhere. One such feature was the use of chrome-plated cylinder bores. This may be technically superior, offering closer running tolerances and longer life (under ideal conditions) but it has the disadvantage that if the bore becomes worn or scored, only a complete new barrel *and* piston will suffice—whereas a

cast-iron liner can be rebored several times, or have a replacement pressed in when its largest oversize has been used.

It was therefore important that the pistons were ideally matched to the barrel on manufacture, and Guzzi barrel/piston sets were given three different sizes to ensure that they were within tolerance. Class 'A' represented 80·000 to 80·006 mm, class 'B' from 80·006 to 80·0012 mm, and class 'C' between 80·012 and 80·018 mm. The pistons were manufactured by Borgo and featured a high dome, although without the usual valve pockets. They carried three compression rings above the 22 mm diameter gudgeon pin, and a single scraper ring at the base of the skirt, which was solid.

The one-piece steel crankcase had steel con-

Rear drive details of the same prototype V7. Note the massive rear hub, seamless silencers and exposed battery

rods with bolt-up big-end eyes running on thin wall split-shell big-end bearings. Like the main bearings, these were made from AL-TIN alloy and were available in various oversizes. The original thickness of standard big-end bearings was from 1·534 to 1·543 mm, and undersize half bearings were available in 0·254 mm, 0·508 mm, 0·762 mm and 1·016 mm. Mains were originally from 37·995 to 37·959 mm in diameter for the front mainshaft (flywheel) bearing, and 53·970 to 53·931 mm for the rear (timing) bearing. Undersizes were made in 0·2, 0·4, 0·6 and 0·8 mm thicknesses. Both the crankpin area and the main bearing surfaces were constructed so that if very slight seizing marks were detected, these could be eliminated using fine carborundum—but if the surfaces were deeply scored or worn oval,

regrinding had to take place before the next bearing size could be used. After a regrind, it was necessary to restore the shoulder relief radiuses, 1·5 mm for the crankpin and 3 mm for the mainshaft at the flywheel end.

Like the crankcase and cylinder barrels, the cylinder heads were constructed in light alloy, and they were each retained by four long and two short studs passing through the cylinders and screwing into the crankcases. Oil tightness was ensured by a paper cylinder base gasket and six cylinder head bolt O-rings per cylinder. The cylinder head gasket was a thick car-type sand-

Prototype in action, with the tester well protected with leather coat and trousers

wich. Each exhaust port was threaded in the alloy to receive a matching screwed nut retaining the exhaust pipe, while the inlet had separate stubs. These were bolted in place with a heat-resistant gasket and three large Allen screws, ready to receive one of the pair of Dell'Orto SS1 29 carburettors.

Easy access to the valve gear on each side was provided by a large alloy rocker cover, inscribed with the Moto Guzzi name and screwed to the head with eight Allen screws and a one-piece gasket. Underneath this cover, a cast-iron one-piece detachable support held each pair of rockers in place. The tappets were of the simple adjuster screw and lock-nut type. The valves themselves were inclined at 70 degrees, and a 34·6 mm exhaust and 38·6 mm inlet were used. These were fitted with single coil springs and

V7 show model pictured at the 1965 Milan Show; this bike had an unusual finish of red/black, with chrome-plated mudguards

seated on special cast-iron inserts.

The camshaft was centrally located between the cylinders, and the base of each pushrod located on a tappet which ran on the appropriate camshaft lobe. The front of the camshaft was connected to the large upper timing gear, part of a matched train of three helical cut steel gears for the timing and oil-pump drive, housed in the timing chest at the front of the engine. The other end of the camshaft incorporated a worm gear to drive the Marelli car-type distributor located at the rear base of the right-hand cylinder.

Engine lubrication was looked after by the three-litre ($5\frac{1}{2}$ pints) heavily-finned, detachable wet sump which acted as an oil tank, and the gear-type oil-pump housed in the base of the timing chest on the left-hand side and driven by the lowest of the three gears which connected to the central crankshaft timing pinion. The pump itself consisted of a pair of gears, with a serviceable width of between 15·983 and 15·994 mm, housed in an alloy pump body. The

Close up showing Dell'Orto SS1 carburettor and Marelli distributor of the 1966 V7 also shown in the photograph below

Below Motor Cycle **journalist Peter Fraser about to ride a V7 in West Germany in November 1966**

only other component was a Woodruff key locating the pump gear shaft in the taper of the timing case gear, where it was retained by a nut and washer.

Pressure in the system was maintained at a constant level by the oil pressure release valve fitted inside the crankcase on the section which supported the sump. This valve was pre-set at the factory to a delivery pressure in the circuit of 2·5 to 3 kg/cm² (35·6–42·7 lb/sq in.) If the pressure rose above the prescribed rating, the

valve would open and restore the correct level. The crankcase itself breathed through a pipe situated on top of the engine, into a metal breather box and then by hose into the atmosphere. An oil pressure switch fitted externally on top of the crankcase, which activated a red oil-pressure light on the instrument console.

The oil pump drew a steady supply from the sump and, after passing it through a wire gauze strainer, delivered the oil through ducts in the crankcase. These directly supplied the oil under pressure to the main bearings, the camshaft housings and the crankshaft, through which it passed to lubricate the big-end bearings. Oil passing out around the big-ends was flung out to lubricate the cylinder walls and the remainder

1967 production 700 V7 under test in Germany; very much a luxurious touring motorcycle with no sporting pretensions. Note clever headlamp mounted mirror

of the engine by splash. The cylinder heads received their own, separate supply through external oil feed pipes.

The big Guzzi's transmission system was closer to car designs, rather than motorcycle practice. Securely bolted to the rear of the crankshaft with six screws was a large-diameter flywheel which also formed the housing for the dry clutch. This consisted of two friction and two plain plates, and eight springs. The clutch assembly was retained inside the flywheel by the electric starter ring gear, that was held in place by eight bolts and spring washers. Passing through the centre of the clutch shaft was a single long clutch push-rod, passing through the input shaft of the gear-box to exit behind the clutch operating lever on the back of the gearbox.

The gearbox housing was bolted onto the rear of the crankcase. It had four speeds and was of the constant mesh, frontal engagement type. The mainshaft was driven by the driving gear on the clutch shaft. All four gears were fixed to the mainshaft—a one-piece assembly. The layshaft was provided with four separate engagement gears, two sliding sleeves and also carried the speedometer drive gear.

The gears were selected directly by the gear

The early V7 engine had several differences from the later models, including carburettors, starter motor and minor engine details

lever—a traditionally Italian heel-and-toe rocking pedal on the right-hand side. This gear pedal controlled the selector shaft which had a toothed sector in mesh with a gear on the selector drum. The drum carried a series of grooves in which the selector mechanism ran, so that its position, and the position of the gears which it selected on the layshaft, was governed by the rotation of the selector. In the drum were five holes, one for each gear, plus neutral, and a spring-loaded pawl ensured that it was positively located in each of the positions in turn as the gear lever was operated. This pawl was drilled and worked additionally as a gearbox breather. The gearbox was also provided with a neutral indicator switch which had an orange warning light on the console to remind the rider not to attempt to start in gear.

Rear drive was by Cardan shaft and bevel gears, again a feature which showed the machine had been designed with a military and police requirement in mind. This took its drive from the rear of the gearbox, via splines on the end of the gearbox layshaft which connected to a universal joint running in a $28 \times 58 \times 16$ mm ball race housed in the end of the swinging arm. The exposed section between the swinging arm and the rear of the gearbox was protected by a rubber gaiter to accommodate the suspension movement. Inside the swinging arm, the universal joint mated up with the drive shaft which ran in two $25 \times 52 \times 16.25$ mm ball races, one at each end. At the rear, this was splined to the bevel drive pinion inside the rear drive box, an aluminium casting filled with EP90 oil to lubricate the drive. The crown wheel was meshed directly with the pinion, and mated up with the rear wheel through an internally-toothed sleeve in the rear hub. The rear wheel could be removed without the need to disturb the drive, simply by removing the wheel spindle and spacer which kept the wheel centred and in mesh.

The V7 was given a sophisticated 12-volt elec-

Factory publicity shot of 1967 V7 production model

trical system, based on a 300-watt Marelli DN 62 N generator located on top of the engine between the cylinders in front of the oil breather box and driven from the crankshaft by two pulleys and a rubber belt. The belt ran down in front of the timing cover, and a large alloy outer casing between the two cylinders down to the base of the timing cover was fitted over the belt, pulleys and the front of the generator to protect them from road filth and the elements. The generator was held in position by a sturdy split metal band and was covered from either side by separate steel pressings.

The generator charged a massive 32-amp hour battery, needed mainly because no kickstarter was fitted and, very unusually for the time, the bike relied entirely on its electric starter. This was a Marelli MT40H motor, a four-pole design with an output of 0·7 hp and rotating clockwise. It was mounted on the rear left-hand side of the crankcase, engaging with the flywheel ring gear via a Marelli IE 13 DA solenoid fitted directly below the starter motor.

1969 757 cc Ambassador, designed for the lucrative American market, during a test session at the Nürburgring. This machine has non-standard panniers fitted

Ignition was again by Marelli, with an S123A distributor that housed a single set of points and condenser. This was driven by a worm on the camshaft and provided sparks via a single Marelli or Bosch ignition coil.

Illumination was provided by a CEV headlamp with a 168 mm lens and a 45/45 watt bulb. The rear light was an oblong alloy-bodied type housing a single 20/5 watt bulb. There were also 3 watt bulbs for the warning lights indicating main and dip beam, neutral, oil pressure, and charging, plus another to illuminate the speedometer. The handlebar switch fitted to the left-hand side was

Ambassador engine details, now with square slide Dell'Orto carburettor and detail changes to the rocker covers, which are now secured by Allen screws instead of the former bolts

the spartan CEV device typical of the period, with an oblong chrome cover retained by two screws. Its simple task was to control the lights, dip and horn—a Marelli type T12 DE/F with screw terminals. There was also a four-way ignition switch mounted in the centre of the instrument console. This selected 0, for off, 1, for stationary parking lights, 2, the running position, when the handlebar switch could also be used to activate the lights, and 3, for starting only so that the key returned to position 2 automatically when released. The electrical system was protected by four 25-amp ceramic fuses.

Like the rest of the specification, the chassis also clearly displayed its government-backed heritage with its heavy duplex cradle tubular frame and equally sturdy swinging-arm. One side of the swinging arm contained the drive shaft

and carried a mounting for the rear bevel drive box. Because of the drive shaft, a conventional swinging arm pin could not be used, so two separate, part-threaded stub spindles were fitted at either side of the swinging arm pivot. These ran on $17 \times 40 \times 12$ mm taper roller bearings sealed from the outside by $30 \times 40 \times 7$ mm oil seals. Side play could easily be taken up by screwing the stub spindles in to tension the bearings.

The 35 mm front fork stanchions were completely enclosed by top covers which also acted as headlamp brackets. These covers came halfway down the length of the forks, and were much longer than the chrome-plated bottom spring covers. Each fork leg only carried one $35 \times 50 \times 10$ mm oil seal, as with full enclosure, no more was deemed necessary. The steering head pivoted on $25 \times 52 \times 16 \cdot 25$ mm taper roller bearings.

In the braking department, on paper at least, the massive full-width 220 mm drums appeared impressive, with a twin-leading shoe set-up at the front. Unfortunately, they were to prove the weak point in the machine's make-up—being hard-pressed to retard the progress of the 500 lb.-plus (in road trim) heavyweight. The hubs were laced to 18 in. WM3 Borrani alloy rims, which carried large-section Pirelli $4 \cdot 00 \times 18$ MTs with a block tread, front and rear.

The remainder of the cycle parts were conventional. One feature was the large, 20-litre ($4\frac{1}{2}$ gal-

A larger capacity Guzzi V-twin prototype of near 800 cc pictured in Italy in late 1969

1967 production model laid the foundations of almost two decades of unbroken manufacture of V-twin models at Mandello del Lario

Below **1970 V7 Special, the European version of the Ambassador model**

lon) fuel tank, which had chrome-plated knee recesses. Twin taps gave over a quarter of the capacity in reserve, and there was a quick-action hand lever filler cap.

Impressive the bike may have looked, but out on the road there was none of the sporting performance of the most famous Guzzis of the past. Having ridden an original V7, I can say with complete confidence that the machine was at heart and in aspiration a tourer in the grand tradition, with a performance inferior to almost every 650 British vertical twin and a top speed of 106 mph. What it did offer was a far higher level of comfort and flexibility, plus an air of quality unmatched by almost anything of the era save BMW.

When cruising sedately at around 50 mph, fuel consumption was in the mid-sixties, dropping down to around the mid-thirties when the machine was used hard. The mechanical noise was low, with induction roar louder than the engine or the exhaust once on the move. But the gearbox was noisy, and with the rear drive layout and the four-speed gearbox, had to be treated with respect. Changing down in anything approaching a sporting manner felt very much as if the rear wheel was locking if the machine was decelerated too rapidly through the lower gears.

But while it was true that the customer who thought that 'Moto Guzzi' on the tank meant that the bike was a sportster would be disappointed, in its element the V7 could be one of the most pleasant bikes to ride, for those who were lucky enough to experience one of the original machines.

It was to be a long wait for most people. Although the first civilian prototype had been shown to the public at the end of 1965, the earliest production machines that customers could actually buy did not begin to appear in dealers' showrooms until the spring of 1967. There was very little change from the prototype, other than minor alterations to cosmetic details—the saddle, with twin grab rails replacing the single one at the rear of the seat, different silencers and rear suspension units, a round rear light, and a headlamp rim with no peak. The prototype had been in silver and black, but this had been changed very slightly, with the tank now in a rich claret although still with chrome recesses, and lined in white rather than black.

The following year, 1968, saw the 700 cc V7 continue, but now with a new starter motor and the carburettors changed to square slide Dell'-Orto VHBs, although these were still the 29 mm size. The saddle had again been redesigned, and now had a hump at the rear to prevent passengers from sliding backwards under acceleration. An oblong rear light like the prototype's replaced the round CEV unit of the previous year. And finally, the colour scheme was changed to white with red lining replacing the silver and red.

1969 saw a bigger change when an enlarged version called the V7 Special was introduced. This had grown to a capacity of 757·486 cc, achieved by increasing the bore to 83 mm while the stroke was unaltered at 70 mm as before. A new type of piston was used—although there were still four rings, the oil scraper was moved up to join the other three above the gudgeon pin and the skirt was relieved to given an almost semi-slipper type appearance. There were still three sizes of piston assembly, but with new measurements. Class 'A' now went from 83·000 mm to 83·006 mm, class 'B' from 83·006 mm to 83·012 mm, and class 'C' from 83·012 mm to 83·018 mm.

The rest of the engine unit showed very little change except for a few minor alterations and improvements. The valves were increased slightly in size to a 36 mm exhaust and 41 mm inlet. They also gained smaller internal valve springs fitted inside the main coils. The clutch springs were changed, too, for a slightly stronger type. The gearbox was the original four-speeder, with identical ratios, but the bevel drive ratios were changed to 8/35 giving a new gearing of 4·375 : 1. Engine oil pressure was increased 3·8 to

The 'Special' was often fitted to a sidecar. The factory even provided stronger fork springs and lower gearing for the rear drive

4·2 kg/cm² (54 to 60 lbs/sq in.)

Despite the limited nature of these changes, the performance was quite substantially increased, with the maximum power up to 60 bhp at 6,500 rpm. Helped by a drop in curb weight from 536 lb (243 kg) to 502 lb (228 kg), this resulted in an increase of maximum speed to 115 mph, with proportionately quicker acceleration.

Two models of the new V7 were produced between 1969 and 1971, when production stopped. As well as the 'basic' Special, there was a version called the Ambassador and intended for the North American market, where Guzzi imports were handled by the Premier Motor Corporation—an offshoot of none other than the Berliner Motor Corporation who over the years handled several of the top European marques, including Ducati, Norton and Zundapp.

The Ambassador was largely the V7 Special with American-market accessories and modifications. These included side reflectors on the mudguards, the round rear light from the 1967 V7 and a cherry red metallic paint job for the tank, side panels and tool boxes. The decals were also changed and there was an 'Ambassador V750' artwork on the side panels. Another American-market modification was the adoption of a sealed beam front light unit.

So the V7 moved into the new decade, much as it had been when first conceived—enlarged, updated, but still at heart a tourer. Now, from these beginnings, there was shortly to emerge a whole range of Guzzi V-twins, based on the original, in many different guises and in three different engine sizes.

3 | V7—a real sports motorcycle

Slim, low and aggressive, the V7 Sport marked a new era for Guzzi, this time with a real sports roadster

When chief designer Ing. Giulio Cesare Carcano retired, and Guzzi appointed his successor, the V7 project gained a man who possessed not only valuable engineering skills, but was also an active motorcyclist—Lino Tonti.

Above all, in Tonti, Guzzi had at last found someone who was capable of successfully assuming the mantle which the legendary Carcano had worn for so long at the factory. To fill the gap left by this great man's retirement was, on the face of it, no easy task. Carcano had been the link with the firm's original chief designer and co-founder, Carlo Guzzi, and during his years in office he had instigated so many brilliant designs that to the casual or uninformed observer it must have seemed impossible to find another man so well qualified to direct the company's design team.

Lino Tonti was perhaps one of the few men who could be expected to live up to the legend—although, in truth, by the time of Carcano's retirement in the late 1960s this was beginning to look decidely fragile. Not only had Guzzi lost the services of one of the finest (if not *the* finest) designers that the motorcycle industry had ever seen, but the company was also experiencing really serious financial difficulties for the first time in its history. As events were to prove, Tonti was to succeed superbly both as a designer in his own right *and* commercially— albeit with the help of Alejandro De Tomaso—in steering Guzzi away from the abyss. Without doubt, the motorcycle which can now be heralded as Tonti's design masterpiece and the machine which spawned the rebirth of the factory was his classic V7 Sport.

Tonti joined Guzzi in 1967, following a decade of assignments with Aermacchi, Bianchi, Gilera and Paton. He had even found time somehow to design the interesting Linto racer—essentially a pair of Aermacchi 250 flat singles on a common crankcase making a twin cylinder 500 racer for sale to the top privateers in international and Grand Prix competition. In fact, it has to be said that this machine was a failure both in terms of performance and reliability, but this was perhaps

more to do with the shoestring nature of the operation than a weakness of the basic design idea—and had Tonti been able to create the same bike with the full backing of a factory, the long-term results might have been very different.

Tonti's first task for Guzzi seemed much more straightforward—enlarging the V7 engine from 703 to 757 cc, and then up to 844 cc. But his own view was that all of this was of somewhat secondary importance, because in his opinion Guzzi's chassis design was not keeping pace with the development of the engine. And as the creator of several of the sleekest racing designs of the preceding years, the distinctly touring, heavyweight character of the original machine was certainly not in line with his own thoughts on what a motorcycle should look like—and handle like!

Designed by Lino Tonti, the sportster was everything the original V7 was not. An amazing transformation of a formerly staid, overweight package

In 1970, after a series of successful record breaking attempts in June and October the previous year (set out in chapter 10), Lino Tonti turned his mind to a plan for the development of the 90 degree V-twin—which was to lead to something lower, leaner, significantly faster and better-handling than any of its predecessors.

His first problem was the height of the Guzzi V-twin engine between the cylinders. This was due to the position of the belt-driven generator on top of the crankcase, reflected in the tall timing cover casting at the front. The difficulty was solved when Tonti substituted the top-mounted generator with a German Bosch G1(R) 14V 13A 19 alternator carried directly on the front of the crank. With a suitably re-cast timing cover, this substantially reduced the overall height along the centre of the power unit, allowing the

whole bike to be reconstructed in a lower, lighter, and obviously much more sporting, mould.

The result was to permit the construction of one of the most beautiful mass-produced frames seen up to that time. It had to be good, for it was a product of Tonti's own personal commitment and effort, the depth of which is illustrated by the story of the designer himself testing a prototype and coming off—breaking a leg in the process. One can but wonder how many other designers of modern times actually get out and

Special high performance version of the V7 Sport . . . called the Le Mans . . . featured race-kitted engine, larger Dell'Ortos, single seat, fairing and triple discs amongst its impressive specification

ride their own products, let alone actually test a prototype!

As well as using an alternator for the first time, the other significant engine modification was a change in capacity. The main reason one can see behind this move was to take advantage of racing regulations, allowing the factory to participate in 750 cc competition. The new engine size was in fact 748·8 cc, achieved by reducing the bore from the 83 mm of the 757 cc version down to 82·5 mm, while the stroke was identical at 70 mm. Higher compression, four-ring, 9·8:1 pistons were used, while a more sporting cam profile, paired coil valve springs, and 30 mm Dell'Orto VHB 30 CD/CD carburettors completed the picture—enabling the new engine to produce a full 52 bhp at 6300 rpm (measured at the rear wheel).

In keeping with normal Guzzi V7 practice, the bores were in chrome, plated directly on the alloy of the cylinder castings, and as before, this meant that pistons were required in three, matched sizes. For the '750' engine, these were class 'A' from 82·500 to 82·506 mm, class 'B' between 82·506 and 82·512 mm, and class 'C' from 82·512 to 82·516 mm.

The engine's drive train used a mix of the best parts from the 703, 757 and 844 cc assemblies. Like the recently announced 850, the V7 Sport featured a five-speed gearbox—although actually it would be more accurate to say that the larger engine made use of the gearbox which had been designed for the sporting 750. As on the

Right **Guzzi factory brochure of 1974, depicting the new 750S model**

Below **Heavily modified standard V7 was one owner's attempt to create his own 'sports' Guzzi. Note Ceriani forks, 1962 Manx Norton double-sided front stopper and bulbous fairing**

**MOTO GUZZI
750 S**

earlier versions of the V7, the gears were helically cut, mainly in the interests of quieter operation.

But whatever technical interest there was in the engine, it was the newcomer's stunning lines which really made enthusiasts the world over drool. Lean, low, racy—it is a style that is as much loved today as when the original V7 Sport first appeared in public at the then bi-annual International Milan Show in November 1971— not only the flagship of the Guzzi range, but the pride of the whole Italian motorcycle industry.

Matching its stunning looks was an equally-breathtaking finish of metallic lime green for the handsomely-sculpted 22·5-litre fuel tank, and triangular side panels. The double cradle frame was in an eye-catching bright Italian racing red, contrasting sharply (and successfully) with the green.

The bike's length contributed to its low, sleek looks, but it really was low, with the seat height at just 29·5 in.—quite exceptional for a machine of its size. The frame and swinging arm consisted mainly of near-straight tubes and the design was masterful, with the result that the same components are still used even today on the latest larger-capacity Guzzi vees. Also brand new were the front forks, which were of Guzzi's own manufacture and incorporated internal sealed damper units—again a lasting Guzzi feature.

With such a low frame, accessibility might

750S, offered in three optional colour schemes. All were basically black, with thick/thin diagonal lines across the tank and panels in red, green or orange

have proved a problem, but to aid maintenance the new frame had fully-detachable bottom rails, a feature for which countless mechanics have thanked Tonti, as it gave superb freedom of access to the engine. At the rear, the mudguard, in stainless steel to match the front, was hinged to allow the rear wheel to be removed without resorting to tipping the machine over.

Although the 220 mm drum brakes were retained from the earlier models, the front was now double-sided with both sides having twin leading shoes. This effectively removed one of the earlier criticisms of the V-twins—poor braking—since not only was the front friction area doubled, but the all-up weight had been reduced. Both hubs were laced to Borrani 'Record' alloy rims with plated spokes—the front rim was a WM2 carrying a 3·25 × 18 in. tyre, while the rear was a WM3 with a 3·50 × 18.

One of the best-liked features of the whole machine was the swan-neck clip-ons, which allowed the handlebars to be adjusted both fore and aft and up or down—one of the few sports machines on which the rider could swap between a touring stance and a racing crouch without excruciating agony in one or both positions. Sadly, the bars also carried one of the least popular aspects of the bike, the period 'snuff box' CEV switchgear.

The rest of the electrics, however, were excellent through the use of the best parts for the job, from a Bosch alternator, regulator, rectifier and starter motor to local products such as the Marelli S311A distributor with twin contacts and condensers, twin ignition coils from the same maker, the powerful Belli high and low pitch horns, and the CEV 170 mm 12-volt headlamp, which had a chrome-plated shell as well as rim.

The first supplies of the new V7 Sport began to roll off the production lines in early 1972, although it is fair to say that they were hardly mass-produced, being in fact almost completely hand-made. Demand was so high in relation to the numbers made that most of the early pro-

duction went purely to meet the hunger of Italy's sporting enthusiasts.

However, some did escape from Italian shores, for a British company, Rivetts of London, had been suitably impressed with the launch at Milan, with the result that they began to bring in small numbers of the V7 Sport (and 850GT) from February 1972 onwards at a price of £1350. Although only a very few were ever imported, customers who did manage to buy one were full of praise, as witnessed by one who actually wrote lovingly about his V7 Sport in an article published by *Motorcycle Sport*, followed by a road test carried out by that same journal.

For 1973, the factory made but one change—to the colour scheme. The striking metallic green and red made way for a far more conservative finish consisting of a red tank and panels with the remainder in black. The previous stainless steel mudguards were retained, and detail relief was provided as on the original by the silver fork bottoms and chrome-plated headlamp, handlebars, grab rail, rear suspension springs, mudguard stays and minor fittings. The complete exhaust system was also in chrome, with the rear end of each Lafranconi silencer cut back diagonally and slashed with three angled slots like a shark's gills.

In 1974, the model was dropped completely, to be replaced by the 750S. Clearly based on the original, there were now some engineering modifications as well as just styling changes. The only change of any significance in the engine saw the factory revert from gear drive in the timing case to using a timing chain and sprockets. Cost was the only reason for this change, and the 750S introduced a system which is still used to this day on Guzzi V-twins.

More importantly, a major modification was the replacement of the massive 220 mm double-sided drum front brake with a pair of hydraulically-operated 300 mm cast-iron Brembo brake discs. Next to the front brake lever was a master cylinder with metal screw cap, and hydraulic hoses connected this to calipers carried on the front of each fork leg.

A change instantly felt by everyone who rode the bike was that the gear change was now on the left. This was to bring the Guzzi into line with American requirements, as by now the 750 sportsters were being sold in the USA. Although the disc-braked 750S had superseded the drum-braked V7 Sport, it was the earlier sportster which appeared when the American magazine, *Cycle* did a 'cafe-racer shoot-out' in their July 1974 issue. In this, they pitted the Guzzi against the 750 Sport and SS Desmo Ducatis, a BMW

R90S, and a Rickman Triumph twin, amongst others. The Mandello V-twin showed up well in such company, and earned the catch phrase 'time drug', highlighting the fact that if a rider just went for a mile ride round the block he would probably never bother with the Guzzi again—but take it out and do 100 miles, then think about the ride, do it a couple of times more, and you risk becoming hooked by the true qualities of the sportster.

There were several other detail changes for the 750S. The seat was exchanged for a new racing-style design featuring a bump-stop, and with room for 1½ people in comfort! Provision was made for mounting a set of Aprilia-made direction indicators, later to become standard equipment. And matt black was used instead of chrome on the silencers, although the exhaust

This clear screen pictured on a 1974 750S was an early attempt by Guzzi at providing a bikini fairing on its sportster; only an extra though

pipes and balancer under the engine were still chrome finished. The latter consisted of two thin tubes crossing diagonally.

The factory offered the 750S in three optional colour schemes. All were basically an overall black, but there were diagonal thick and thin stripes slashing down the tank and side panels, and the customer could choose from either red, orange or green for this detail. The side panels themselves were the same pressings as those on the 850 tourer of the same vintage, and were likewise lockable, but they carried a pair of 750S badges.

An ignition-activated electric petrol tap was fitted on the right with a conventional tap on the left, which also acted as a useful reserve. But the tap, together with an hydraulic steering damper, were two items which seem out of place on an otherwise 'no-gimmicks' sportster. Quite frankly, the tap was only one more thing to go wrong and would be very expensive to replace, while the hydraulic steering damper was little more than redundant with such a fine-handling bike, and only served to make the steering heavier than it need have been. Good for racing, perhaps, but on the road. . . .

Except for these two questionable features, I think that the British *Motorcyclist Illustrated Road Test Annual* summed up the 750S nicely when it reported 'that unlike other, or at least the majority of sports classics, the 750S is also highly practical'.

The final version of the Guzzi 750 was the 750S3, launched at the same time as the touring 850T3; it utilized many of the latter's components, including the linked braking systems

Timing gears on the V7 Sport, replaced by cheaper sprockets and chain on 750S/S3

Although the factory claimed a top speed of 130 mph, neither the 750S nor its predecessor, the V7 Sport, were capable of this in standard trim. Okay, with the factory race kit, yes they were, but in standard 'showroom' guise, Guzzi's 750 sportster was hard pressed to nudge a genuine 120 mph—although an outrageously optimistic Veglia speedo made even the factory's claims seem conservative. Buried in the tank, the true maximum was between 119–121 mph, depending on the rider's weight.

If racing performance was what you were after, the racing kit was what you needed. The full kit, for Formula 750 racing, comprised a hot

camshaft, 36 mm carburettors, an open exhaust system, and straight-cut close-ratio gears. With all these fitted and the cylinder ports bored and gas-flowed to match the larger carbs, plus a fairing, maximum speed went up to between 132–134 mph.

The final version of the Guzzi 750 was the 750S3, launched at the same time as the 850T3 in early 1975. The S3 looked much like the 750S at first glance, and was finished in the same colours—its fuel tank came from the 750S, but the side panels were from the T3 and fitted with '750-S3' badges. Several of the most noticeable parts were off the 750S, including the front and rear suspension, silencers and balance pipe, mudguards (hinged at the rear), seat and grab rail, hydraulic steering damper and adjuster—but sadly, the popular but expensive swan-neck handlebars had gone to be replaced by cheaper, non-adjustable clip-ons. Virtually everything else including the main part of the engine, the electrics and wheels (with the patented triple disc linked braking system) came straight off the 850T3.

Mechanically, in fact, the 750S3 owed more to the touring 850 than it did to either the V7 Sport or the 750S, and for the technical details of the design, the reader is advised to consult the next chapter, dealing with the 850 engines. Except for the barrels, pistons, carburettors/ manifolds, crank, and clutch flywheel, the whole drive train was pure T3. The cylinder heads were T3 castings which retained the exhaust pipes with bolt-up clamps rather than screwed ring nuts as on the earlier 750 sports models, this meant that new exhaust pipes (in the V7 Sport 750S shape) were needed. This was actually a considerable improvement, because the old nuts had a habit of working loose, and if allowed to 'chatter' in the port, would ultimately ruin the thread in the head casting.

As on the 850T, there was no replaceable air filter element—just a large rubber connecting the carburettors but not the breather box. The lack of an air filter as such was to lead to bad press for Guzzi in road tests of both the 750S3 and 850T for 'loud induction noise, which was higher than the level of mechanical noise', as one tester correctly stated.

The new sportster made its debut in Britain at the same time, in May 1975, as Guzzi's new British importers, the Luton-based Coburn & Hughes group. At that time, it was the most expensive Guzzi ever imported, at £1749—but this price remained unaltered during the 18 months in which the model was available to British enthusiasts. It is believed that around 200 were brought in up to October 1976, when supplies dried up with no more forthcoming from the factory after the introduction of the new 850 Le Mans model.

If one is fortunate enough to be able to compare a 750S3 with the 750S, it becomes all too apparent that the two bikes have much more than a production run to separate them. For a start, the riding position on the S3 was compromised by the loss of the adjustable swan-neck clip-ons and the substitution of fixed clip-ons that were too far forward and too low for most purposes, plus a new position for the once well-placed footrests that took them much further forward. The result could prove agonizing

for a rider who was anywhere under six feet tall. And as *Motor Cycle* found when they tested the S3 in 1975, performance was not as good as they had hoped, with a maximum one-way speed of 115·8 mph and a mean (two-way) figure of 114·2 mph. They did, however, find some of the machine's other features more impressive— notably its stopping power, for 'any bike that can pull up in 24½ ft from 30 mph has to have good brakes', and its handling was to match, for, 'the bike is rock steady at speed with plenty of ground clearance'.

Even though the basics owed much to its touring counterpart the T3, the 750S3 did manage to retain the low, lean, aggressive look of an uncompromising sportster, shouting 'performance' from every angle. It was a style at which the factory showed themselves to be masters, and it was a wise decision whey they used it to even greater effect and created the S3's replacement—the highly successful 850 Le Mans. Above all, the S3 and the 750S that preceded it had proved the viability in both sales and production terms of creating a sportster cheaply and simply out of an engine and a large number of parts from the less glamorous touring models. It was a principle that Guzzi were to put to use again and again.

4 | T series

Neither the 703 nor the 757 cc versions of Guzzi's 90 degree V-twin had proved sufficiently powerful to make the various V7 touring mounts anything other than willing, reliable performers. Certainly, the main criticism levelled at them by factory testers and the motorcycling press alike had been their lack of zest.

To counter this, the factory again enlarged the engine size, but this time it was by lengthening the stroke, rather than increasing the bore as they had done to turn the original 700 cc V7 into the V7 Special/Ambassador series. Now, the familiar V-twin was a nominal 850, with a new stroke of 78 mm, but the same bore of 83 mm—giving an actual capacity of 844·06 cc. The pistons had three rings instead of the four-ring type used before, and with a 9·2:1 compression ratio, the power output was increased to 51 bhp at 6000 rpm. The rest of the engine was much as before, with only a few minor improvements, but it now gained a five-speed transmission.

The new, larger capacity Guzzi was first shown to the public in the factory's usual way, at the Milan Show in November 1971—appearing in two versions, the V850GT and the GT California. The latter was an update of a model which had first appeared on sale that year, in Europe only, powered by the earlier 757 cc engine. And in fact, both bikes were virtually the same machines as their smaller predecessors. The only changes to the 850GT apart from the power unit and transmission were extremely superficial. It gained Aprilia flashing indicators, chrome-plated mudguards and a new style of tank and panel decals. The decals were now in white and consisted of '850' above a 'GT' logo, plus a large 'V' flanked by horizontal lines. The small toolboxes behind each of the large side panels carried simple, matching horizontal double lines.

The California package was much more striking, although not completely new. Clearly its styling was an attempt to emulate the American Harley-Davidson, and perhaps to steal some of the latter's charisma. Even the name was obviously selected to convey the idea that its potential buyer was about to experience a piece of Stateside West Coast excitement and brashness (even if he happened to live thousands of miles away on another continent). In V7 form, the idea had already proved itself successfully, and like that other italianization of an American

genre, the spaghetti Western, the concept was to continue to be a best-seller throughout the 1970s—even though the later California models were little more than dressed-up 850 T3s.

The original California 850 could also be said to have been simply an 850GT with accessories bolted on, but this was a somewhat different package from the later 850s, which used the T3 frame, forks and linked brake system. The original 'Cali', as it was soon dubbed, was a no-compromise custom cruiser—fat and ugly, or sensuous and beautiful, as your taste dictated.

The full-dress style consisted of a large, four-point, toughened perspex screen, laid-back high

First model to sport a capacity of 844 cc in the Guzzi catalogue was the 850GT, first shown at the Milan Show in November 1971

and wide western bars, a black and white buddy saddle adorned by a wrap-around rail, rear carrier, 1950s-style Harley-type panniers (but in fibreglass), plus front and rear chrome-plated crashbars. The result was a motorcycle which perhaps came closer than any other manufacturer could achieve (except Harley themselves) to the 'American dream machine'. Unlike the metallic cherry red and black of the GT, the California was black and white, which, with the large areas of gleaming chrome, gave it the final touch of eye-catching distinction.

Both of the new 850s went on sale in early 1972, and besides proving popular with the dis-

Original California was based on the early V7 concept. The overall styling was very much more a no-compromise custom cruiser than the later T3 based model

cerning enthusiast at home, both the GT and California were exported to several other countries almost from the beginning. These included the USA, Scandinavia, Germany, Holland, France . . . and Britain.

1972 was the first year that the Guzzi V-twin was imported into Britain, when, as described briefly in the previous chapter, Rivetts of North London brought in a very limited number of both the V7 Sport and 850GT, selling the larger machine for £1145, including purchase tax. But soon, in 1973, a new importer was appointed. This was Barretts of Redhill, headed by Don Barrett who had been involved in the early 1960s with importing the Capriolo range of lightweight motorcycles into Britain. During 1973 and 1974, Barretts imported several different Guzzi models—including both the GT and California.

1974 was the last year that the 850GT/

Eldorado and V7 California were available, in this final year all three were fitted with a single 300 mm cast-iron disc operated by a Brembo caliper mounted at the front of the offside fork leg, another change was the fitment of British Lucas direction indicators.

1974 marked an important point in the evolution of the large-capacity touring Guzzi V-twin. This landmark was the 850T, a machine which was to transform both the image and the actual ability of what had, up till then, been a large-capacity motorcycle of strictly limited appeal. Before, the Guzzis' buyers had been purely touring riders, those who were content to travel at a leisurely gait and who had little interest in using their machines in a sporting manner. The 850T changed all that.

Here was a machine which retained all the softer attributes of the original, but also offered its rider the handling and roadholding abilities of the highly-acclaimed V7 Sport model. Not only that, but the new package which went on sale in the summer of 1974 offered many subtle refinements that gave it a much wider appeal. The 850T ushered in a new era for Guzzi, that of the large capacity *sports/tourer*.

It is true to say that the 850T owed much more to the V7 Sport than it did to the V7 touring line. Not only did it use the Sport's frame and suspension, but it also incorporated much of the engine design and specification of the 750S, a new development of the V7 Sport which also went on sale in 1974.

1974 California was the final variant of the 'fat' V7 to appear. For its final year, a Brembo disc front brake replaced the previous drum

One innovation shared by both the new models was the adoption of hydraulic disc front brakes. The new brakes were made for Guzzi by Brembo, but although the 750S sportster mounted a twin disc set-up, the 850T was only equipped with one of them. At the rear, it retained the 220 mm drum of the earlier models, but now had a finned brake plate and twin-leading shoe operation. The 850T's brakes were, in fact, its chief weakness compared with the 750S or the later 850T3, for the performance from the single 300 mm cast-iron disc and forward-mounted caliper on the right-hand fork leg was best described as wooden. Not only was the brake just not powerful enough, but worse still, it lacked

850T, a clever marriage of a soft engine and race bred handling. The first of the Guzzi sports/touring models appeared in mid-1974

feel and called for too much hard pressure. An additional brake disc and caliper conversion kit was soon made available (as part number 17.92.30.00) to convert the 850T to twin front discs—a modification which is highly recommended.

The remainder of the 850T closely followed the specification of the V7 Sport and 750S detailed in the preceding chapter, with only small changes to the engine and chassis.

The main difference was that although the 850T's engine had a family likeness to the 750s, it used the larger engine dimensions developed for the 850GT and California. But proving that the 850T was intended for more serious sporting work, the chrome cylinder bores carried the higher compression 9·5:1 pistons, and the camshaft profile was the same as used in the 750S (and identical to that used later in the Le Mans!)

In traditional Guzzi V-twin practice, the piston assemblies were matched to the barrels in 'A', 'B', or 'C' sizes, with crankshafts and con-rods colour-coded either blue or white.

Together with larger, 30 mm Dell'Orto VHB 30 carbs, this modified engine not only gave more power—53 bhp at 6000 rpm—but a much crisper performance resulted from the improved power-to-weight ratio offered by the lighter chassis.

The 850T (and 750S) engines were the last of the V-twins to employ the wire-mesh oil filtration system introduced on the original V7, so were not designed to carry the car-type oil filter cartridge used on the later models. But just before the 850T was taken out of production in 1975, the last batch constructed were fitted with the improved system designed for the T3 and 750S3 engines. This required a new sump.

Externally, the most obvious change between the 850T's engine and the units fitted to the earlier GT/California was the replacement of the belt-driven Marelli generator. Previously, the position of this atop the crankcase between the barrels had meant that the front of the engine was dominated by a large alloy outer casing. Now, like the V7 Sport, the 850T employed a much neater (and more effective) Bosch 180-watt alternator mounted at the front of the engine and encased in a round, projecting polished alloy cover held in position by four Allen screws.

Much of the balance of the electrical equipment was also changed to bring the 850 into line with the V7 Sport. Many of the new parts were

This 850T, with sidecar, was built by Norwegian enthusiast dealer Maarten Mager. It had Wasp forks, 230 mm 41S Grimeca front brake and knobbly tyres

also of Bosch manufacture, although exceptions were the lighting and switchgear, the Marelli S311A distributor (now with twin contact breaker points and condensers), and the twin external Marelli HT coils, placed out of the way under the tank.

The headlight was a 170 mm Aprilia unit with a separate Bosch 40/45 watt bulb, but as the usual practice, the USA market models were fitted with sealed-beam units of the same rating. Both the headlamp rim and the shell were chromed, like the Aprilia direction indicators. Together with a larger, more 'square' CEV rear light, all these parts were simply 12-volt versions of the fittings from the 250TS two-stroke twin

Same outfit as previous page, showing an amazing display of lean (and riding ability)

introduced the same year.

The various changes to the electrical system offered a considerable advancement in the new 850T's specification, and the new switchgear made the electrics both more reliable and more controllable. The four-position ignition switch was similar to that on the V7 Sport (which had five positions) and was a type used on many Italian cars of the period. There was also a set of four warning lights for neutral (orange), ignition (orange), charging (red), and lights (green). These were mounted on a black-painted cast alloy plate bolted to the top fork yoke and which also carried the instruments on either side of the lights—a Veglia mechanical rev-counter which replaced the earlier electronic type, and a matching speedo, both of which were inscribed with the Moto Guzzi emblem.

The majority of the cycle parts were 750S, but the specification was rather more comprehensive. Both stainless steel mudguards were designed to give more protection against the elements, and although the front looked similar to the 750S's that machine's hinged rear guard was changed for one of more conventional appearance. Front and rear wheels carried WM3 Borrani alloy rims, shod with 3·50 × 18 front and 4·10 × 18 rear tyres. There was a pair of front crashbars, centre and prop stands, and lockable tool boxes behind the side panels—unlike the later T3 models which had only decorative panels and no carrying capacity.

A comfortable riding stance was ensured by the near-ideal relationship of footrests and controls, which, combined with a low, almost flat handlebar bend and an extremely spacious and well-padded dualseat equipped with a sensible grab rail meant that many hours of comfort in the saddle could be enjoyed by rider and passenger alike. A large-capacity, 25-litre fuel tank plus excellent economy ensured that the machine's long distance touring comfort could be explored to the full.

There were three colour options for the 850T, although in each case, the main colour was used only on the tank and side panels. Buyers could choose between brown, red, or a very attractive metallic green. A unique feature of the model was the use of metallic gold tape to decorate the tank and panels—a feature which regret-

Cylinder barrels, pistons and gaskets from 850 series engine (some had 4-ring pistons)

tably clashed with their air of quality given by the rest of the machine. The tank also carried metal 'Moto Guzzi' badges (as did the V7 Sport, 750S and 750S3) rather than transfers, and there were matching metal '850-T' logos for the side panels.

Despite quite a short production life span, the 850T sold well both at home and abroad. In North America, the importers for the USA and Canada, the Premier Motor Corporation, advertised the new sports/tourer in double page colour advertisements which carried the heading 'The machine built exclusively for unlimited touring, in style—a masterpiece of elegance and craftsmanship'. Although this clearly originated from an American advertising agency, it conveyed the impression which the factory was keen to promote—that Moto Guzzi meant a quality product.

In Britain, the model actually had two importers. The first was Barretts of Redhill, who imported a mere handful in August 1974. However, this effort was soon to be completely overshadowed when the factory appointed a new importer the following spring—the Luton company Coburn & Hughes, who already held the Ducati concession. Coburn & Hughes unveiled five Guzzi models at a ceremony held on Thursday 8 May—a line-up that included not only the 850T, which had been increased in price from the 1974 figure of £1346 to £1479.50, but also the new 850T3 and T3 California, neither of which had previously been seen in Britain, and had only just been launched in Italy. The other

Basking in the sunshine, 850T3 on test during July 1975 with Motor Cycle **magazine**

two models were the 250TS and 750S3.

The T3 was priced at £1599.50, and the T3 California at £1699. The extra £100 bought a package which included a toughened, tinted Perspex screen, a pair of braced, laid-back western handlebars, a hydraulic steering damper, knee protectors on the cylinder heads, a black and white 'buddy' seat with chrome grab rail, lockable fibreglass panniers on substantial frames, and a chrome-plated carrier, front and rear crashbars. The 'Cali' specification was completed by a pair of rider's footboards, a set of revised controls which included a heel-and-toe gear lever, and an effective prop stand which could be operated by the rider from the saddle.

Both the T3 and the California were clearly based on the 850T, but the biggest difference was in the braking system. For the first time, the new models carried Guzzi's exclusive, patented integral triple disc set-up. This was rightly claimed to provide more stopping power and braking safety than any conventional system on a production roadster ever before.

Applying the footbrake pedal did not only operate the rear brake in the normal way, but instead, it applied *both* the 242 mm rear disc brake *and* the 300 mm left-hand front disc brake. The braking pressure was automatically balanced to produce the correct bias needed to bring the rider to a steady, even stop. For emergencies, or simply to hold the bike while stationary, the front brake lever could also be used to apply the right front disc only. The

850T3 California, based on the standard T3, but with screen, 'western' bars, 'buddy' seat, crashbars, panniers and lots more, circa 1975

front master cylinder had been changed for one of smaller capacity, which had a plastic cap instead of the previous metal item. Unfortunately, this was not an improvement, because the cap was prone to split if the owner inadvertently overtightened it.

There were several other, but less significant, changes. Attention had been given to improving the oil and air filtration for the engine. The disposable car-type oil filter which had been tried on the latest 850T was housed in the sump, so that both this casting and its gasket were revised. And for the first time, the Dell'Orto carburettors had a disposable paper air filter—vitally important for an engine employing chrome-plated cylinders

Non-standard British Pantera fairing and panniers fitted to a 1976 850T3 California

which could not be rebored.

The Bosch alternator now had an increased output, at 280 watts. Although the headlamp was still an Aprilia product, it now had a black-painted shell. The USA version with its sealed-beam had a rim twice as deep as the European one, and a thick rubber gasket between the rim and the shell. The idiot lights and instruments had a plastic console in place of the alloy type, and the ignition switch now had three instead of four positions. The clutch cable also incorporated a cut-out switch, which meant that the engine could not be started unless the clutch lever was pulled in.

Other changes included handlebars some four inches higher than before, and rear suspension units with either three or five pre-load adjustment positions—the three-position type had built-in operating handles. The side panels

were retained by rubbers and were no longer lockable. Also, the shape of the exhaust pipe and the design of the balance pipe running under the engine were changed.

The California was only available in black with contrasting white stripes (now transfers and not metalfoil as on the 850T), but the T3 was offered in a range of colours including salmon red, dark green, black (with white or gold stripes), and metallic ice blue. It was also available later in a few other colours, including dark brown and silver.

Several of the T3s supplied to the British importers during 1975 and 1976 were to the USA specification. The latter year also saw the introduction of an economy version of the California, which by this time had had its UK price increased to £1799. This 'cheap' version, known as the California Rally, sold for the old price of £1699 and had white painted mudguards and a large speed-ometer (like the V1000) with no rev counter.

On the road, although the T3 offered a similar performance to the 850T, it was a better balanced machine—if only for its superior braking performance. Like the T, it had a true top speed of 117 mph (the factory quoted 124 mph). Having owned a couple of T3s and ridden many miles on them, while being fortunate enough to ride all the other large-capacity Guzzis, I honestly feel that although it had neither the crowd-pulling looks of the California nor the street-racer lines of the Le Mans, the T3 is in my opinion the best of all the 850s—even including the the later T4. I found it possessed abilities that few other

T3's first major update came in 1979 when several cosmetic details were introduced, changes including cast alloy wheels, SP seat and CEV headlamp

The T4 introduced in 1980 was essentially an economy version of the Spada NT, but with smaller engine

bikes could match—the California and Le Mans included—of being able to 'eat up' the miles. The only major flaw (my ownership dated from 1975 to 1977) was that of inferior finish.

But for sheer riding enjoyment, I still remember both my T3s with affection. How do you describe a bike which handles superbly, but at the same time soaks up all manner of road surfaces, is economical—I used to obtain 60 mpg on a regular basis—has braking which could literally be employed with both hands off the bars from the eighties down to almost zero, with a level of comfort found on very few other bikes, and a near-ideal riding stance?

When *Motor Cycle* tested the T3 in their 26 July, 1975 issue, tester John Nutting was full of praise with comments like 'the bike was strong, quiet and clean as ever, even though it had covered the previous thousand miles without opening the tool kit or wielding a rag. In addition, I felt as fresh as when I'd started out earlier that afternoon. That sort of performance puts the £1600 Moto Guzzi right at the pinnacle of the world's best tourers. Of its handling, he had this to say, 'Most un-Italian, they (Guzzi) haven't opted for ultra-taut steering. Helped by the low centre of gravity of the in-line engine, Guzzi have given the bike a pleasing ability to be flicked through bends. The steering is light and almost telepathic—you're almost through a corner before you think about it'. *Motor Cycle* summed up by saying, 'With its price tag, the Moto Guzzi is a high class, long term proposition, a practical machine built for a purpose. It is dif-

A brand new California, the 'II' made its debut at the Milan Show in November 1981

ferent, but that is one of its very charms. In all, a classic motorcycle, worthy of the name Moto Guzzi'.

What a road test report cannot show is what a bike is like over a long period. The engine itself was the model of reliability, but with the T3, like other motorcycles, there *were* faults. Besides the poor (for the price) finish, I do know several

owners who suffered problems with leaking fork oil seals, rear gearbox drive seals, an occasional rectifier failure, and flimsy switchgear. One of the common weak points was the lack of durability

In many ways the California II was somewhat of a return to the styling of the 850GT California, with its fatter appearance and deeply valanced mudguards

of the various rubber components. Any deficiencies which there might have been in the quality of the original material or moulding was aggravated by the factory themselves, who insisted during most of the time that I was a Guzzi dealer, on spraying a preservative onto the bikes before they left the plant. Whatever this might have done to benefit the metal parts was outweighed by the damage it did to the rubber it contacted, literally rotting such items as the handlebar grips and footrest rubbers.

The factory offered a range of accessories for

the T3. These were mainly fittings which were already supplied as standard on the California, but from its earliest days, the Guzzi V-twin had proved a popular machine with sidecar enthusiasts. And starting with the T3 series, the factory officially recognized this by offering optional heavy-duty front fork springs with special rod end caps to locate the bottom of the spring. There was also a kit to lower the final drive gearing, consisting of a pair of 6/32 ratio bevel gears for the rear hub, a special universal joint, and a matching sleeve to connect this and the bevel shaft.

The USA model T3 was known as the 850T/3FB, and carried small, additional 'FB' stickers in white just under the '850-T3' badges on the side panels. Physically, the only changes were the usual American-market sealed beam headlight, side reflectors and a modified handlebar light switch with CEV indicators replacing the Aprilia ones.

The T3's first major update came in 1979 when several cosmetic changes were made. The most important of these was the introduction of cast alloy wheels of the type already in use on certain other models including the SP (Spada) and Le Mans. The later, oblong rear light used on these two bikes was now fitted to the T3, along with a Spada seat, a lockable filler cap, Spada switchgear, a CEV headlamp and indicators, an improved centre stand, and a black plastic cover over the alternator replacing the polished alloy one. A tribute to the soundness of the original design was that mechanically it remained unaltered.

The California was also updated, but less so, receiving only the locking petrol cap, plastic alternator cover, CEV headlamp, and the Spada switchgear.

The following year, the T3 became the T4, but just to confuse the issue, the original T3 also remained in production—albeit on a reduced scale—ultimately only to be discontinued completely in 1982.

The T4 was very much an economy version of the Spada NT, with the smaller engine. The power unit was virtually identical to the T3 in most respects, but had Nickasil bores instead of the chrome-plated type which had been used on the 850 series since its inception. The silencers were Spada items, and the T4 now came with the Spada handlebar fairing as standard, plus a Spada seat. The centre stand, another Spada part, was much simpler to operate, and Spada rear indicators were fitted to match those in the fairing. The front brake calipers were remounted behind the fork legs.

The new T4 was not only a practical touring motorcycle, but also a most attractive one—although its only colour scheme was a deep wine-red shade for the fairing, tank and side panels, with gold lining. To mark its close rela-tionship with the T3, the tank and panel badges remained as before, with the exception of the number '4' supplanting the '3'.

The next development was when a brand-new version of the California appeared at the Milan Show in November 1981. This was a strange mixture of old and new, with a return to an appearance not dissimilar to the original V850GT California of the early 1970s, while its engine was updated by using the square 'slab' style cylinder heads and barrels first used on the Le Mans III.

Like the Le Mans III, the new machine, called the California II, was substantially different from

The T5 was largely the work of the De Tomaso controlled styling shop in Modena, rather than the company's traditionalists back at Mandello

the machine it replaced. Not only was its detail specification and appearance changed, but its engine was enlarged to 948·81 cc. Putting the California into the 1–litre class was achieved in the same way that it had been with the V1000 and G5, by increasing the bore to 88 mm. The main reason for the capacity increase was fashion, but a useful spin-off was the improved torque figure, now 7·7 kg/m at 5200 rpm.

At the time of its launch, the factory claimed a maximum speed of 118 mph, but in truth, with all the standard accessories in place, it was barely able to reach 105 mph. Not only this, but at around 90 mph, or sometimes a little less,

depending on road and wind conditions, an unnerving weave would set in. This was also a problem on other Guzzis using the large windshield, which in my experience simply created too much wind resistance over 80 mph to be practical for high speed work—and the California's panniers probably merely aggravated the situation. However, against this can be set its ability to combine, at low to medium speeds, a sweetness of handling and road-holding with an American laid-back style.

The California II was launched on the British market in March 1982. The price was £2899, but by two years later, this had risen to £3599. Unlike the T3 California, buyers could choose from two colour options of either dark chocolate or white, with red and yellow stripes for the tank, central sections of both mudguards, and the side panels. The latter carried a California II sticker in place

1985 850TS. Changes from the earlier model were 18 inch rear wheel (formerly 16 inch), screen, tank carburettors and colour scheme

of the previous metal badge.

One specification difference was the swinging arm of the California II which had been increased to 470 mm between centres and was additionally braced.

The California II benefited from the factory's improved machining equipment, which enabled tighter tolerances to be used. Along with the use of aluminium rocker supports, this gave a much quieter engine—and the addition of the improved air filtration pioneered on the Le Mans III, plus the less noisy exhaust system, made the larger California even more civilized than before. Like the 850 California, the II proved a good seller, and factory records demonstrate that style has consistently triumphed over function with both this machine and the Le Mans outselling the standard versions, the T3 and T4.

In an attempt to update the now aging T4,

Guzzi introduced the T5, which initially proved to be perhaps one of the most unpopular of all the Guzzi V-twins.

The T5 was largely the work of the De Tomaso controlled styling shop in Modena, rather than the company's traditionalists back at Mandello. Largely because many enthusiasts tended to shun the model, and because of its poor reception by the press, disappointing sales followed its launch.

One of the main claims made at the time was that the T5 had been the victim of too little market research—and testing. Certainly the use of 16 in. wheels front and rear seemed at first glance a move to 'modernize' rather than for any real practical purpose. Around this centred one of the main areas of criticism made by press testers—lack of sufficient ground clearance.

Because of this the factory was forced to bring out a revised version in the spring of 1984. This featured several changes including an 18 in. rear wheel, the frame from the recently announced Spada II, a screen for the miniature fairing and several smaller modifications.

Actually when I tested both the original and modified versions of the T5 in May 1985 I was pleasantly surprised—and impressed—enough to begin to wonder if many press testers are more impressed by speed and acceleration graphs, rather than what a motorcycle is like to ride and use everyday. . . .

All 850 series engines had sprockets and timing chain, unlike the early V7 and V7 Sport models

5 | Le Mans—fast shaft

Of all the production bikes to leave the Mandello, del Lario factory in the last decade, the Le Mans is unquestionably the best known. It has also proved consistently to be a best-seller since its debut at the 1975 Milan Show, even though at the time it was the Benelli/Moto Guzzi 250 fours which stole the headlines.

Named after the famous French endurance racing circuit, the Moto Guzzi 850 Le Mans was clearly aimed at the enthusiast with street racing aspirations. But there was more to the Le Mans than this, for it could attract the sporting rider who might have been considering a Laverda or Ducati, but needed a bike with civilized enough manners to double as a tourer. Unlike machines such as the 3C or 900SS respectively, the Le Mans could do both equally well. In fact, when I was a dealer for both Ducati and Guzzi I used to keep the 900SS and Le Mans side by side in the showroom and I was often asked by customers which I would choose. I would reply, 'Well, if you want to ride the bike every day, pick the Guzzi, but for Sundays only use, choose the Ducati'.

Compared to its predecessors, the 750S3, 750S and V7 Sport, the Le Mans showed a clear advantage in terms of its marketing appeal, although many traditional Guzzi enthusiasts would say that the original V7 Sport was the bike which incorporated the real heart of an out-and-out sportster, a theme which had become a shade watered down by the time that the Le Mans appeared. Nevertheless, Moto Guzzi was a commercial operation and it was the Le Mans, not the V7 Sport, which achieved the most sales success and was to remain in production for a much longer period—so in this instance the marketing men scored a victory over the technical department.

None of this is to say that the Le Mans was not a fine sportster, because in so many ways it was. But where the 900SS, the 3C and the V7 Sport offered a raw, animal appeal that kept the rider constantly extended, the Le Mans lacked this sharp edge, possessing instead an infinitely more subtle charm.

Technically, the new sportster drew heavily on both the 750S3 and 850T3. In fact, the engine assembly and transmission was essentially only a tuned version of the touring 850—with identical cylinder dimensions, gearbox and final drive. To achieve the extra performance needed in its new role, the Le Mans had higher compression pistons (10·2:1), larger valves (37 mm exhaust, 44 mm inlet), a more sporting camshaft profile and a pair of Dell'Orto PHF 36 pumper carburet-

tors with large plastic bellmouths.

At the time of the Le Mans' debut, it was reported that this engine unit was giving a massive 81 bhp output at 7600 rpm, good for a maximum speed of some 134 mph. In reality, the truth of the matter was rather less on both counts, since the power output was 71 bhp at 7300 rpm and 124 mph was the best that a rider would get out of this. Even so, the engine performance combined with the Le Mans' surefooted handling, excellent braking and aggressive style at last gave Moto Guzzi a motorcycle with which the factory could take on all comers in the superbike stakes.

The prototype on show at Milan clearly laid down the Le Mans' distinctive lines, which more than echoed the S3 on which many of the cycle parts were clearly based. When the first produc-

The original Le Mans (subsequently nicknamed the Mk I) is to many *the* finest version of the classic Italian motorcycle

Left **The American version of the Le Mans (I) featured an 'extended' headlamp out from the fairing amongst a few other minor differences from the European version**

Below **Lakeside shot of a Le Mans (I) taken in June 1976**

tion bikes began to arrive in dealers' showrooms, the model's early promise was clearly fulfilled, for its sporting stance was reflected in every detail. With clip-ons, rear set footrests, a racing-style bump stop saddle, bikini fairing, drilled discs, matt black frame and exhaust system, and silver cast alloy wheels, this was a machine whose every line stated—speed.

Befitting the name and image, the machine could be bought in a bright racing red finish, but it could also be supplied in a metallic light grey/blue (a few were even available in white, from

Right **The Le Mans II used a full fairing of similar design to the SP (Spada), with instrumentation to match**

Below **Even though the LM (I) had proved a consistent best-seller, the factory replaced it with the more angular Mk II, which made its debut at the West German Cologne Show in September 1978**

March 1977). But above all it was the red, applied to the tank, mudguards, side panels and fairing which really enhanced the Le Mans' appearance. Even though the fairing had a distinctive orange 'dayglo' section below its tinted screen and surrounding the 170 mm headlamp, somehow this unlikely colour combination contrived only to further the image.

The machine's more civilized aspects were subtly subdued. Although direction indicators were fitted, they and their support arms were finished in black, blending more easily into the

contours of the rest of the machine than would normally have been expected. Pillion footrests were provided, but it was a strictly intimate affair, unless the passenger actually sat on the padded seat hump.

The seat was altogether a distinctive feature of the Le Mans, and could have been both a stylistic and ergonomic (for one person only!) coup. As it was, the seat was to prove one of the few poorly-designed items on the whole bike. The interesting thing about the seat was the way in which it was moulded so that the nose extended over the rear of the tank, a curiously effective design feature which should have also enhanced rider comfort. The problem was that the whole thing was moulded in one piece from foam rubber which simply was not strong enough for the job, with whole chunks of foam actually breaking away—particularly from the poorly-supported

front section. A favourite and practical remedy was to fit a seat from the earlier 750S3 model.

Another part which was more than likely to let the bike down, certainly in northerly climes, was the battery—a miserable 12-volt 20 amp hour affair, compared to the 32-amp hour type fitted to the other models. After extended use with lights on, such as might well be encountered in a typical cold, wet British winter's riding, this frequently failed completely to get the bike going. Without a back-up kickstarter, and with a bike which was far from being easy to bump start, quite often the irate Le Mans owner was simply stranded.

Such annoyances apart, the Le Mans soon won a loyal and enthusiastic following, for here at last was a *practical* Italian super sports bike. So maybe the 900SS did have the edge out on the open road, but what of it, for the Le Mans rider knew who would have the last laugh the next time there was some town traffic to negotiate.

When it was launched onto the British market in June 1976, the Le Mans cost £2000, some £400

The major distinguishing feature of the North America only CX100 was the side panel labelling, although some may notice a change in carburettor on this bike

more than the standard T3, but there was no shortage of eager buyers. Much of this must have been due to the attentions of the motorcycle press, who were almost unanimous in according the Le Mans rave reviews. Some of these testers, it was felt, had been sold on the bike simply by a 'round the block' ride, but there were those who even went continental touring. One magazine report which definitely came into the latter category was the one prepared by *Motor Cycle Mechanics*, whose editor Colin Mayo and features writer, Bob Goddard, (on a Le Mans and 850T3), took part in an extended three-day, 1400 miles marathon over unknown roads through six European countries.

From the outset, this looked to be a less than cheery prospect with, as they put it, 'the cafe racer Le Mans promising to be uncomfortable over the twelve hours we proposed to ride each day, and the T3 touring version gasping to keep up . . . or so we thought! Even the gallop back from the importers in Luton to Peterborough when they collected the bike was found to be a bit of an anti-climax. Perhaps expecting too much, Colin Mayo summed up his feelings; 'after all, the Le Mans did look as though it would crack the sound barrier and gobble up Z900s on the way. While it definitely had a bit more mid-range surge than the 750 (S3) version, the overall performance was only slightly improved and the

A 'UK special', the black/gold Le Mans was listed by the British importers simply in a successful ploy to remove stocks from the warehouse in readiness for a new version, the Le Mans III, at the end of 1980

gearchange was just as crunchy and awkward as ever'.

Harsh words, maybe, but as the test wore on, the two riders found more and more to praise. It was soon found that the Le Mans could live with the T3 as a touring mount, thanks to its 'fat spread of powerful torque' and that it could handle, too, for 'there could be no doubt that the long, low Le Mans would go round bends quite a bit faster than many of its Oriental contemporaries, and took to sweeping roads like a duck to water'.

The test was summed up as follows. 'The Le Mans never really felt as though it were trying, despite the rapid nature of our journey, and the lop-sided rumble of the big V-twin motor had a relaxed feel to it. The luxury of not having to lubricate and adjust the chain is a strong bonus. But in many ways the Le Mans is a showpiece to be admired and envied and is not nearly so inspiring to ride as it looks'. *MCM* concluded by saying the important thing was that the Le Mans was very different to the norm and that it thus captured the same exotic aura that Ferraris and Lamborghinis thrived on.

Thoroughbred it might be, but it was neither nervous, nor highly-strung. Throughout the test the Le Mans averaged 44·5 mpg despite maintaining an average speed of almost 60 mph for the whole trip. This can often be bettered by an owner, even though many would use it as a sportster rather than a tourer. Its lazy style was

'Working' prototype for the LM III was this factory hack using Mk I cycle parts, pictured in 1979

sometimes to fool even the most hardened road testers into thinking that the Le Mans did not have too much bite to its performance, but as a later chapter will show, it often proved to the unsuspecting opposition in production machine racing that it had rather sharp fangs.

Even though the Le Mans had proved to be a consistent best-seller, Moto Guzzi decided in early 1978 that it was time to think about updating the design. The result was to appear in September of that year at the Cologne show in West Germany as the Le Mans II, one of only two new Italian bikes—the other being the pre-production Ducati 500 Pantah.

The Le Mans II's most obvious change was the adoption of a Spada-style three-piece full fairing, which gave the whole bike a more angular look. At the same time, the Le Mans had gained most of the fairing-mounted equipment from the Spada. This included the complete instrument layout and switchgear, including the quartz clock and voltmeter. The large, moulded rubber dashboard was suitably re-inscribed 'Le Mans'. The front indicators were now integral to the fairing, and the clip-on bars were changed to suit the fairing's upper section. The red finish was as before, except that there was now more of it, and the frame continued to be painted matt black. But the metallic blue/grey and white were dropped, and royal blue became the other colour option.

Le Mans III was a major redesign—new fairing, tank, seat, panels, exhaust system and modified engine top end were just some of the many changes

Above **The cylinder barrels, heads and rocker covers of the LM III were sharply angled in appearance, compared with earlier models**

Left **Le Mans III instrumentation layout was totally dominated by the massive white face 100 mm Veglia tachometer**

It was reputed that the power output had been improved and that the exhaust system had been changed. This was not in fact true, for the changes were cosmetic only. But improvements were made to two of the main shortcomings of the early Le Mans. The troublesome single saddle had already been changed during 1977 for one which gave a true two-up capability and also did not fall apart, despite still being constructed from a similar material. And although the very first Le Mans IIs had the old-type battery, this was very shortly uprated to 32-amp hour. There were several other minor changes. Amongst these, the front brake calipers were relocated at the rear of the fork legs, which were now finished in black rather than silver. The ignition switch and rear brake master cylinder cap had been changed for the improved SP type, the latter linked to an idiot light when fluid gets low, and some other details were similarly brought into line.

Out on the road, the paper performance of the fully-faired Le Mans was not noticeably different from the original. The British magazine *Motorcycling* recorded a maximum (prone) speed of 126·89 mph and an average of 48 mpg. Tester Charles Deane faulted the switchgear, stand operation and a firm dualseat, which 'did little to absorb road shocks and lifted only just enough to reach the toolkit beneath, it also didn't lock!' But overall, he remained favourably impressed with the Le Mans II, in particular for its ability to match many 1000 cc bikes in performance and beat them in fuel economy. I, too, found the Mark II not to have any real performance advantage over the 'Mark I', but its fairing and increased level of equipment offered an improvement in terms of comfort and convenience. There were many, however, who still felt that the naked early model had the edge on appearance.

In late 1980, a number of modifications were all introduced at the one time on the Le Mans II. The chrome-plated cylinder bores were replaced by Nickasil ones. The internal fork dampers

The German importers offered a '1000 cc' version of the Mark III; illustrated here with twin headlamp fairing and bellypan in 1983

(manufactured by Lispa) were improved, and the forks were converted to air-assisted operation. Rear suspension was also changed, with the substitution of Paioli proprietary units.

At the same time, a 'UK Special' was introduced onto the British market. This was the Le Mans II in an overall black and gold livery, gold being used for the wheels, fork bottoms and pin striping on the black areas of the fairing, tank and side panels—altogether very much a Guzzi copy of the Ducati 900SS of the period. The importers marketed the machine simply as the Le Mans Black/Gold, and at a price which had by then risen to £2999. Of course, there was a reason for the introduction of this special model, which was quite simply to remove stocks from the warehouse in readiness for a new version, the Le Mans III.

This was not just a lightly-modified adaptation of the previous Mark, but constituted quite a major rethink on the theme. In particular, the engine received several updates. Most noticeable of these was the introduction of new, square finned cylinder heads and matching Nickasil-bored barrels. Although such things as the camshaft profile and the size of the valves remained unaltered, and even though the compression ratio was actually decreased from 10·2 to 9·8:1 (a move intended to improve low speed running and torque), the performance was still improved by 3 bhp while the torque went up to 7·6 kg/m at 6200 rpm.

This was quite extraordinary, because it was achieved entirely by the combination of better machining equipment improving tolerances, the use of aluminium rocker supports (which also helped to quieten the tappets) and an improved air filtration and exhaust system. The last of these was the most extraordinary achievement of all, for whereas it is generally easy to increase performance by adopting a less restrictive but anti-socially noisy exhaust, Guzzi's designers had contrived a system which was not only more effi-cient, but was actually quieter than before! Guzzi's 'performance exhaust' was so good at its job that it actually enabled the Le Mans III to become the first European motorcycle to comply with the stringent European CEE 78.1015 regula-tions governing noise, as well as international anti-pollution standards. The double skin ex-haust pipes and silencers were now chrome-plated.

The fairing was another big change from the Le Mans II, with the new wind tunnel-tested design having rather smaller dimensions than before. There was also a form of spoiler offering deflection of the air current past the underside of the fuel tank and the top of the cylinder heads. Guzzi claimed that the result was greater speed with less fuel consumption. In fact, they quoted a maximum speed of 143 mph (230 km/h) and a dry weight of 453 lb (206 kg). Had this been true, it would have been a fantastic improve-ment, but in reality the top speed with the rider buried in the tank was a maximum of 135 mph. Although less impressive, this was still definitely

Late in 1984 the official Le Mans 1000 appeared. Revised styling and engine tuning—and of course increased engine capacity—added up to an impressive bike with a maximum speed of over 140 mph

quicker, but how much of it was due to the streamlining and how much to the mechanical changes it is difficult to tell.

Inside the fairing, pride of place was given to the large (100 mm diameter) white-faced Veglia racing tachometer. This was flanked by a speedometer on the right, voltmeter on the left and rows of warning lights below. These, together with the ignition switch, were housed in a thick rubber console, as were the two triangular green indicator warning lights. The handlebar switchgear was taken directly from the Mk II.

Like the Le Mans II, the III had a square headlamp and square indicators. But on the redesigned fairing, the indicators were now mounted externally on the extreme outer edge of the moulding. This was a very vulnerable position and in fact any slight mishap would not only

damage the indicator, but the fairing itself as the moulding was locally weakened.

The frame, forks and wheels remained basically unchanged, but the swinging arm was substantially lengthened by a total of two inches. More noticeably, perhaps, the whole appearance of the bike was altered by a new tank, seat and side panels. With the long-distance rider in mind, the tank capacity had been increased from 22·5 to 25 litres. The seat looked similar to the Le Mans II, but now had a new, colour-moulded rear section. Below the redesigned side panels, a prominent feature was the adoption of new mountings for the footrests, with both front and rear rests

Styling of the Le Mans 1000 was very much in the vogue of the V65 Lario four-valve sportster, introduced a few months earlier

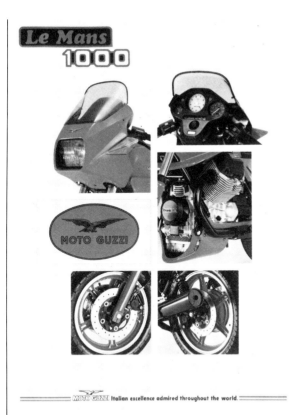

1985 Le Mans 1000 brochure, showing various aspects of the machine

now carried on a cast alloy latticework in place of the former tubular steel brackets.

The colour-finished parts were now painted either red, metallic light grey/blue, or white. Not only did these colours hark back to the original version of the Le Mans, but there was even a reintroduction of the orange dayglo strip on the fairing—albeit much reduced in area. Although the side panels still carried moulded badges, now stating '850 Le Mans III', the tank and fairing were given transfers instead. The designs for these were the 'eagle' and 'Moto Guzzi' in gold with a black outline. The fairing carried a black stripe as well as the dayglo panel to give it a flared look.

The next move, and the latest machine to join the Le Mans family, came in late 1984 with the

introduction of the Le Mans 1000. Like the V1000, SP and California II, this model took over the 948·8 cc version of the V-twin engine, but with a higher state of tune to uphold the Le Mans' sporting tradition. The valves were both 3 mm larger than on the 850 engine, at 47 mm inlet and 40 mm exhaust. The compression ratio was upped to 10:1 and the bike used 40 mm Dell'Orto carburettors and new exhaust pipes of the same diameter. The silencers were also a different pattern, and both they, the header and balance pipes were finished in gloss black chrome. The net result of the new engine and ancillaries was a power output of 86 bhp at the crank, and a top speed quoted at 141 mph (230 km/h).

A 1000 cc Le Mans was not altogether new, though, for a batch of such animals known as the CX100 had, in fact, been sold in the USA in 1978/79. Due to some quirk in emissions regulations it was found necessary to fit the 1000SP engine into the Le Mans clothing. Precise details of just what a CX100 was are hard to clarify because a variety of bits and pieces were fitted depending where they were on the production line. Suffice to say, the batch was small and the machines are simply analysed as Mk II Le Mans with 1000SP engine. Also a year before the 'Mk IV' the German importer, Motobecane, sold his own '1000 Le Mans III' complete with bellypan and twin headlamp fairing.

The bike's styling was very much in the mould of the V65 Lario, itself deriving its lines from the V35 Imola II and V50 Monza II. Unlike the earlier Le Mans, there was much more use of the main colour (red), including the wheels and the bottom, detachable frame tubes. A bellypan was incorporated below the fairing, following the fashion of the mid-1980s, which by then saw the Italians following the Japanese style lead rather than vice versa.

For the first time, certain engineering basics of the Le Mans were changed. Notably, the front wheel followed another fashion trend by going

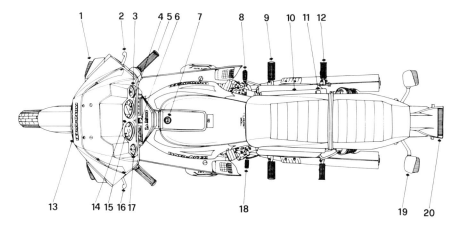

down to 16 in. The rear stayed at 18 in. but gained a new, wider 130/80 V18 tyre, with a matching 120/80 V16 front. The brakes were still the patented linked disc system, but were now a uniform 270 mm all round.

Fairing and aerofoils were closely related to those of the Le Mans III, but the front indicators were now sharply angular and in fact doubled up as quite effective wind deflectors for the rider's hands. The instrument console was unchanged from the Le Mans III, and was also adopted by the Lario. Different parts which the Lario gave to the Le Mans included the switch-gear, foam rubber handlebar grips and the dog-leg control levers. Windtone horns replaced the components used from the earliest Guzzi V-twins.

Only time can tell whether the latest and biggest Le Mans is as successful as the original 850 in all its various developments. But one thing is certain, and that is that 1000 cc model continues to typify the same unique formula, a blend of the sporting and the sophisticated. After ten years, the Le Mans still preserves the relationship between a fire-breathing sportster and everyday practical motorcycle that first endeared it to the rider with his head in the clouds but his feet firmly on the ground.

Line drawing showing control details and other items of the Le Mans III from the factory workshop manual
1 **Front turn signal lights**
2 **Control lever, R/H front brake**
3 **Voltmeter**
4 **Speedometer**
5 **Throttle control grip**
6 **Ignition key**
7 **Fuel tank lock**
8 **Left front brake and rear brake pedal**
9 **Front footrest**
10 **Master cylinder for left front and rear brake**
11 **Saddle lifting lever**
12 **Rear footrest**
13 **Headlamp**
14 **Panel**
15 **Rev-counter**
16 **Clutch lever**
17 **Clock**
18 **Gear selection pedal**
19 **Rear turn light**
20 **Tail light**

6 | Automatic—too few converts

Moto Guzzi traditionally had a reputation for promoting innovation, and their introduction of a large capacity motorcycle with shaft drive and automatic transmission was no exception. When the V1000 I-Convert was launched into the superbike era of the mid-1970s, it was the only one of its kind. And subsequently only Honda, with special versions of their 400 twin and 750, have tried to tread anything close to the same path.

The V1000 project came about as a result of De Tomaso's automobile background. In the car market, automatic gearboxes were an accepted 'luxury' fitment filling an important and profitable sector of the buying public's requirements. If this was true for cars, why should the same not be true for bikes? With this unassailable logic, De Tomaso committed an important sector of Moto Guzzi to proving what has so often been shown to be the case, that things which work in the four-wheel industry are often a failure on two. While automatics aid everyday car driving, the majority of motorcyclists select their chosen bike for totally different reasons from those which motivate the average car driver. It was this fact which De Tomaso failed to appreciate when launching the V1000—although if it was a mistake, he was in good company, for even the mighty Honda organization failed to recognize how automatics would be received.

Like most automatic cars, the automatic Guzzi was closely based on an existing, manual gearchange model—in this case, the 850T3. As is also the case with many automatic versions of cars, it was given a larger capacity than the manual-geared bike. The Convert also gained several touring extras from other models in the Guzzi range, including the T3 California's tinted screen, panniers, footboards, sidestand and crashbars. Outwardly the only brand new parts were the seat, grab rail, rear light and tail fairing, the instrument console, front master cylinder, and miniature aerofoils mounted on the front crashbar. But of course, the real innovations were out of sight, tucked away behind the engine and gearbox casings.

The engine was essentially the same 90 degree V-twin which powered the 850 models, but with the cylinder bore increased from 83 mm to 88. With the stroke remaining the same as the 850s

at 78 mm, this gave the new engine a capacity of 948·8 cc. On a 9·2:1 compression ratio, the maximum power output at the crankshaft was 71 bhp at 6500 rpm but a lot less at the rear wheel, with the torque converter consuming several bhp alone. Unlike the chromed bores of the earlier V-twins, the pistons of the Convert ran in steel cylinder liners. Although the factory still adhered to their method of matching the original pistons and cylinders on new machines, with Class 'A' between 88·000 and 88·009 mm, and Class 'B' from 88·009 to 88·018 mm, the use of solid liners meant that for the first time it was possible to rebore the V-twin engine. For this purpose, oversize piston assemblies were available in 0·4 and 0·6 mm sizes.

The con-rods and crankshaft were the same type as the post-1972 850 engines following a spate of broken rods which had resulted in the stroke being increased from 70 to 78 mm; and similar care went into matching these at the factory, depending on the crankpin diameter. Fac-

V1000 I-Convert on show just prior to it entering production. A pointer to its pre-production status is the 'inked in' logo on the rocker cover

Top **De Tomaso (and the press) misjudged the mood of the bike buyer with the V1000 automatic, just as Honda did with their 400 and 750**

Above **A disassembled torque converter, bought in by Guzzi from the German Sachs company**

tory markings were put on each con-rod and on the flywheel side of the crankshaft shoulder. Blue markings indicated a crankpin diameter between 44·008 and 44·014 mm, while white was for a pin between 44·014 and 44·020 mm. Under-size split bearing shells were available in three sizes—0·254, 0·508 and 0·762 mm. The remainder of the bottom end was virtually the same as it had been on the 850, although the camshaft was modified to accommodate a drive for an automatic transmission fluid pump—the profile remained the same—and the timing cover was also modified. Because of the larger cylinder bores, the crankcase mouths into which they fitted had to be enlarged, although the cylinder base gaskets remained the same.

There was even less modification to the top end of the engine—just a new type of cylinder

Engine details of the V1000 including, in the centre of the picture, the cooler for the hydraulic torque converter fluid

head gasket and different jets in the carburettors. The heads and 30 mm square slide Dell'Orto VHBs were otherwise the same as those fitted to the T3. Externally, the only visible modification was the minor addition of a pair of knee protectors in the form of small, oblong rubber pads on brackets which bolted to the cylinder heads.

All of these changes, of course, were insignificant compared to what had happened to the clutch and gearbox assembly—and this was where the bulk of the V1000's design work and R&D budget had gone.

Strictly speaking, the system which Guzzi used was not a true automatic gearbox, but such it was labelled at the time by the world's press, and the term has stuck. In fact, it was a form of semi-automatic transmission, based on a type of hydrokinetic torque converter (hence I-Convert

or Idro-convert), bought in as a unit from the German Sachs company. This was fitted with a two-speed gearbox on which the ratios could be selected with a heel-and-toe lever operated by the left foot. To complicate matters, in theory at least, there was also a clutch, but its sole purpose was to swap between the two ratios—unlike a conventional gearbox, where it is also necessary for the clutch to be used to allow the engine to take up drive. On the Guzzi, this function was taken over completely by the torque converter. And since, in practice, changing ratio was virtually redundant, the machine was to most people as nearly automatic as made no dif-

The V1000G5 was simply a manual version of the automatic model, with conventional 5-speed gearbox and revised controls

ference, its speed being entirely controlled by throttle and brakes.

The torque converter itself was a sophisticated development of what is sometimes known as a fluid flywheel (or, less politely, a slush box). These names are apt because they approximately describe its operation, in which the transmission medium is oil, a fluid. Instead of there being a direct link through the transmission as in a conventional system, the fluid provides a slightly 'loose' connection and a gradual take-up—somewhat akin to the effect of slipping a friction clutch, but without the problems caused by doing this all the time. In effect, it provides a sort of continuously-variable transmission ratio, within the limits of the design specification.

On the Moto Guzzi, the maximum converting ratio (akin to a gear ratio) was 1·60:1. The other end of the scale was a direct 1:1 drive. The overall size and shape of the converter itself can best

be visualized by imagining two deeply-dished dinner plates mounted so that their rims are touching. Picture the inside of this divided so that a hollow chamber is formed all around the circumference in the shape of a cylindrical channel like an endless sausage. The inside of each 'plate' is further divided up by radial vanes, so arranged that they direct the flow of liquid passing between them into a spiral, coiling as it circulates in the channel. And this spiral flow passes through the third element of the design, which looks like a small multi-blade fan, free to spin between the two plates.

In the real torque converter, this whole assembly is sealed and filled with fluid. The first 'plate' is called the impeller; this is fixed to the crankshaft and rotates to act as a pump for the hydraulic fluid. The 'fan' is called the turbine; this is fixed to the gearbox input shaft and its function is to accept the hydraulic drive from the impeller. The remaining 'plate' is called the stator, and is mounted on a one-way clutch so that it is only free to rotate in the same direction as the other components. It is the stator which is the key to the efficiency of this unit.

To see how the system operates, it is best to consider what happens as the machine moves away from a standstill. At first, the impeller, which is connected to the revolving crankshaft, is the only part which moves, although in doing so it also stirs up the hydraulic fluid. As the revs start to rise, the impeller begins to revolve at a speed much greater than that of the other components and the fluid is pumped around the spiral in the endless circular chamber. As it passes from the impeller through the vanes of the turbine, it starts to impart drive to the turbine, before passing into the vanes of the stator. Here, it attempts to push the stator backwards but cannot do so against the one-way clutch. Instead, the vanes redirect it to the impeller so that it can repeat the whole cycle. Because this redirection process imparts extra drive, the action in fact increases the torque transmission in a similar way to the low gear of a conventional gearbox.

Once under way, the speed of the vehicle starts to increase. The unit continues to operate in the manner described so far, but gradually the speed of the turbine rises closer to the speed of the impeller. As this happens, the angle at which the fluid hits the turbine blades changes, so that it is directed with less and less force against the vanes of the stator. So long as there is a speed differential between the impeller and the turbine, the stator is locked against its one-way clutch, increasing the amount of torque available (the output). But as the turbine speed approaches that of the impeller, the stator starts to move off its one-way clutch and the torque effect reduces

like that of a variable gear ratio. Finally, as the speeds equalize, all three components rotate together, resulting in a kind of 'lock up' and giving straight-through drive. Of course, as soon as the machine is accelerated, the engine revs rise again, speeding up the impeller and starting the whole process again as happened when moving off from rest.

On the V1000, the entire torque converter assembly was housed in the flywheel, occupying the position previously used by the clutch plates on the conventional engine. The flywheel housing, together with the starter ring gear which bolted onto it, were special items for the Convert.

Simply incorporating a torque converter in such a way, however, would inevitably cause an early failure for a reason which may not be obvious from the description of the unit given so far—the converter is not 100 per cent efficient. At best, when it is locked, it approaches 95 per cent, but when acting as a converter it may be less than 90 per cent. All forms of transmission introduce some losses, so this is not a problem in itself, but the lost energy is dissipated in the form of heat, which *is* a problem. The waste heat has to be shed in some way, and the Guzzi's designers arranged for this by allowing it to be carried away by the hydraulic fluid. Instead of simply sitting inside the converter, the fluid was circulated by a pump.

The pump was housed in the front of the engine on the specially-modified timing cover. From there the fluid passed through a pipe leading to the machine's converter fluid tank situated under the left-hand side panel, which then supplied the converter itself through another pipe. After circulating through the converter, the fluid continued through a pipe leading to the base of a cooling radiator mounted across the front of the frame front downtubes. Passing out of the radiator through a union at the top left-hand corner, another pipe then took it back to start the whole cycle once more.

G5 model offered riders an improved performance (with the same engine specification) compared with that available from the automatic V1000

The converter fluid tank had a capacity of 1·7 litres, and it was recommended that the level should be inspected every 300 miles, while it had to be changed every 18,000 miles. The recommended lubricant was Dexron ATF (automatic transmission fluid). Its circulating pump consisted of an inner and outer rotor and associated components, and took its drive from the end of the camshaft. The pressure in the system was controlled by a fluid pressure relief valve, also located in the timing cover, adjacent to the pump, and calibrated to allow a running pressure of some 1·8–2 kg/cm² (25–29 psi).

Despite the wide spread of ratios available from the converter, it could not substitute for the whole range of a conventional gearbox or provide all those necessary to suit every driving condition. So the system adopted on the Guzzi also incorporated a choice of two overall gear ratios—and in order to swap between them, it was necessary to retain an orthodox clutch. But unlike the normal Guzzi car-type assembly, the Convert's clutch was a specially designed dry multiplate set-up of a type much more common on other marques. This rode behind the torque converter so that the clutch centre was mounted on the torque converter's outer housing and had an integral shaft passing through the centre to take its drive from the turbine. The clutch plates and outer clutch drum were located in front of the gearbox, housed in a specially-recessed area of the casing.

There were seven friction and five plain steel clutch plates, with six springs which were standard T3 items. Unusually, these were assembled 'back to front', with a pressure plate located behind the plates which were actually retained in their housing by a large circlip which fitted in after them. The operating pushrod and lever assembly were unlike those of manual Guzzis.

So, too, was the gearbox. This had just two ratios; 1st speed (low), with 18/24 teeth gears giving a 1·33:1 ratio, and 2nd speed (high) with a 1:1 ratio from a pair of 22 tooth gears. Like the conventional manual unit, this two-speed semi-automatic gearbox had a one-piece mainshaft with both gears attached and a separate layshaft with detachable gears. There was also a single sliding sleeve mounted on the layshaft which mated up to the gear control (selector) fork. This in turn was mounted directly onto a gearchange shaft which passed through the gearbox casing and led via a series of linkages and rods to the heel-and-toe gearchange lever—toe down for low ratio, heel down for high gear. The primary drive to this unit was originally by straight-cut gears, later changed to helical type to quieten gear whine experienced on the early models, with a ratio of 1·57:1 from 19/22 gear teeth.

The shaft final drive followed conventional Guzzi V-twin practice, but with a different universal joint which had a long extension at the

Bend swinging on V1000G5 whilst under test in Britain during 1979

rear to take up the place of the intermediate drive shaft used to connect the universal joint to the bevel gears on the other models. The rear bevel drive ratio was 9/34 teeth.

The net effect of this transmission train was rather more energy-sapping than a conventional manually-geared model. Despite the larger engine, in high ratio the top speed of the V1000 was only 108 mph. But then, for the type of rider at whom the machine was supposedly aimed, this was probably expected to be entirely adequate.

The frame was Moto Guzzi's well-proven and good handling full duplex loop with split bottom rails, first seen on the V7 Sport and later on most of the other models including the 850T/T3 series. Most of the cycle parts, in fact, were common to the T3 and V1000, including the front and rear

Unlike the V1000 automatic, the G5 provided its rider with a rev counter as well as its large speedo, albeit one of miniature proportions

suspension, and the spoked, alloy rim wheels. The stainless steel mudguards were identical—as were the painted steel side panels, except for their V1000 I-Convert badges. The fuel tank was outwardly the same, but incorporated a fuel gauge which fitted up into the offside front of the tank and activated a warning light on the instrument console.

The latter was new to the Convert. Mounted on the clamps of the standard T3 high handlebars, it was a large, square-section black plastic casing moulded in two parts. The centre of the console was given over to a larger Veglia speedometer—no tachometer was fitted, for none was really necessary with the automatic transmission. On either side were a mass of warning lights—five per side—and a pair of flick

switches. Apart from these, the black CEV indicators and the large, oblong rear light, the electrics were standard Guzzi V-twin fare.

The handlebar controls were straight T3, but on early models a triangular master cylinder was fitted to the brake lever operating the right-hand front disc brake. This had a small, circular metal filler cap with a screwdriver slot to enable it to be unscrewed from its recessed housing. On later models, after 1976, this was replaced by the standard round master cylinder used on the other twins.

As well as the wheels, the Convert used the same rear cush drive as the T3, with its twelve separate rubber cush vanes. It also adopted the linked braking system with triple Brembo discs, but on early models the discs themselves were different.

The multiplicity of warning lights on the Convert's instrument console reflected a particular interest in 'safety' features on this model. To warn of low fluid level, the rear brake master cylinder cap incorporated a switch, and another

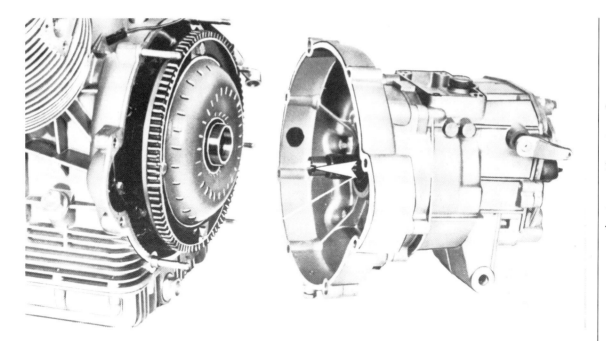

On the V1000 automatic, the clutch was situated between the gearbox and converter. This workshop manual illustration shows how the engine with starter ring gear/converter was bolted up to the gearbox (and clutch) assembly

switch linked to the prop stand prevented the engine from being started until the stand was raised. When in use, the prop stand also activated a mechanical brake caliper, enabling the rider to park the V1000 on a hill. This system was cable operated and worked on the rear disc brake.

Because of these features, combined with Guzzi's linked hydraulic brake system and the V1000 transmission's own unique contribution to comfort and safety, it was awarded the 1975 Premio Varrone—a top Italian award presented annually to the most technically interesting and aesthetically beautiful production machine in the country.

My own riding impressions of the V1000 recall an uncanny experience of having so little to do and at the same time feeling so remote from the main action. Somehow the big Guzzi felt more similar to a grown-up automatic moped, than a conventional motorcycle.

The first time you approached a corner at speed and shut off, it felt more as if you were driving a two-stroke car, than a large capacity motorcycle. This had nothing to do with the linked brake system, but the divorced feeling given by not having to change down a gear combined with no real braking effect from the engine.

Similarly, when rolling to a halt, there was no need to grab the clutch lever or dab into neutral. As the revs dropped to a tick-over the converter relaxed its grip and the fluid idled round ready for the next getaway.

Perhaps a motorcycle that you just got on and rode with none of the traditional rider functions, added to a lengthy list of devices which needed time to familiarize with made the V1000 just too unfamiliar for its own good.

Three basic choices of colour scheme were offered on the V1000—black, silver and metallic ice blue. Black could be had with a choice of gold or white striping, applied on the tank, side panels, panniers, rear light cover and the front crashbar aerofoils—the other two colours had black striping on all these parts. The plastic louvres on the side panels were left their natural matt black, and all models had black painted frame, swinging arm, fork yokes, headlamp shell, number plate support, footboards, hydraulic steering damper and centre stand (the side stand was cadmium plated). The front fork bottom legs were in silver. Model identification was by metal badges on the tank ('Moto Guzzi' in white on a black background) and the side panels. These carried a special V1000 I-Convert logo, picked out in polished chrome with a large '1000' against a black background, and the rest, smaller, against red. The words 'Moto Guzzi' were also on the panniers, where a transfer was placed halfway up each side panel.

The V1000 was launched on the Italian home market in the spring of 1975. It was exported shortly afterwards, with the first models to reach Britain arriving in July of that year, less than two months after the appointment of new concessionaires, Coburn & Hughes. At the time, both C & H and the press saw the V1000 as the exotic flagship of the Moto Guzzi range, but in reality things never worked out like that, and although the Convert was listed by the factory until 1984, sales were never anything more than steady to a decidedly limited market. In fact, British sales were so poor that the importers stopped bringing them in after 1977.

De Tomaso believed in it, the press loved it, and, although few, its buyers swore by it. So what went wrong with the V1000? In retrospect, the first real failure of the new management following the De Tomaso takeover. Quite simply, it was this—that in the real world of motorcycles, only the buyers dictate sales. The Convert was heralded as a major new motorcycle on account

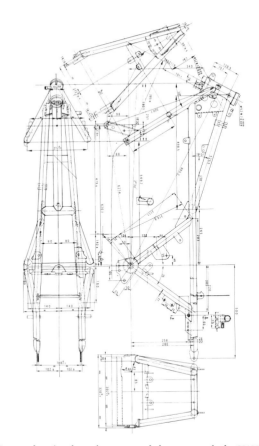

Frame drawing from factory workshop manual: the V1000 automatic and G5 both used the same basic chassis as the other Guzzis, including the T3 and Le Mans

of its automatic transmission, full touring equipment, new and exciting safety features—plus an engine 100 cc larger than any previous Guzzi. But where it counted, on the sales floor, it turned out that the customers' perception of the value of these things was quite different from what the pundits had expected. De Tomaso had made the classic mistake of so many manufacturers—that of *assuming* what the customer wants, rather than finding out exactly what *is* wanted, by actually asking!

7 | SP or Spada—the motorway express

Wind tunnel performance dial—competitor to Big Ben . . .

With the SP, known as the Spada (sword) in Britain, Guzzi set out to offer a viable alternative which could break BMW's virtual monopoly of the long-haul, luxury touring market. For although the existing 850T3 was close to a BMW-style package, as a flagship it fell short in several important respects of the standard set by the top-of-the-range German flat twins. Most importantly, it lacked the engine capacity of the R100 series—it also lacked the sophistication that typified the Teutonic twins, and compared to the German company's flagship, it lacked the purpose-designed weather protection of the RS fairing.

At Mandello, in mid-1976, Guzzi's management were convinced that it was necessary for the company to embark on a major expansion, with the expressly stated policy of increasing production two-fold by the end of 1978. To achieve this, it was essential for Guzzi to break into new sectors of the existing motorcycle market, so it was logical and attractive to try and borrow a share from BMW. Thus the plans were laid for what was to emerge as the 1000 cc Guzzi SP (Spada).

It was an entirely logical step for Guzzi, for although brand new designs like the lightweight four-cylinder machines and the middleweight V-twins (the V35/50) were well advanced, the luxury tourer drew very heavily on existing technology and could be put into production after only a short development period. In fact, so far as the main chassis and engine parts were con-

A more modern 300 hp electric motor now powers the wind tunnel propeller, formerly driven by a Piaggio aero engine

cerned, the Spada was largely a marriage of the components from the T3 and V1000 models. The increased engine capacity necessary to give Moto Guzzi a competitive machine in the important '1000' class made use of the work already carried out on the 948·8 cc unit devised for the V1000, described in the previous chapter. This was simply given a conventional clutch and gearbox, courtesy of the T3, and housed in a frame and suspension package that was again comprised of existing components from the 850 machine.

But if these measures smacked of pure convenience engineering in order to boost the otherwise outclassed T3 into a larger capacity arena,

this was because the bulk of the R&D budget was concentrated on those areas in which BMW had previously so clearly outgunned Moto Guzzi. Mandello's planners correctly perceived that their basic engine and chassis were already sound enough, so it made both economic and practical sense to aim for the rider who bought BMW because of the high level of standard equipment and rider protection afforded by the flat twins. Concentrating on these two areas alone meant that the new model could be developed in a much shorter time, and sold at a much lower price, than would have been possible with a completely new bike. Thus the first priority was to equip the machine with an efficient, factory-matched fairing as BMW had done with their RS model.

In many ways, it was surprising that Moto Guzzi had not done this before, and that they had had to take the lead from BMW. For it was Guzzi who originally led the world in the development of motorcycle streamlining, when in 1950 they became the first factory in the game to construct their own wind tunnel at Mandello for testing the works racers. It was therefore odd that the factory which had been amongst the first to recognize the importance of aerodynamics in competition had not followed this into their roadster production, but had allowed their test facility to stand idle for almost 20 years, with its massive Piaggio aero engine, rated at some 2,000 hp, gathering dust.

With the inception of the Spada project, this was no longer to remain a silent reminder to the greatest days in the factory's history. The mighty piston engine was pressed into service once more and its roaring slipstream was unleashed into the task of finding the best compromise between protection and style in the design of a fairing for the new flagship. Besides the aircraft engine, a marine engine from a torpedo boat was tested, but this proved unsuccessful. For the majority of the SP project and afterwards, Guzzi finally decided to replace the aging aero engine with a more modern 300 hp electric motor, which is still in use today.

Several ideas were tried before the final selection of the SP's streamlining was made — a choice which, as time was to prove, was a decision well taken, as variations of the original design have been used from then until the present day with only minor changes being necessary. By the standards prevailing at the time, Guzzi's solution was elegant and somewhat unconventional. Even though the streamlining gave the protection of a full fairing, the design was actually closer to the traditional combination of a separate handlebar fairing and legshields. But where these fittings earned themselves a reputation for a utilitarian ugliness that was the antithesis of good style, the Guzzi version of the theme was all that they had never been — modern, stylish and aerodynamically efficient.

The thinking behind the design was impeccable. The separate top section could turn with the handlebars, allowing it to be mounted much closer to the rider than a conventional full fairing, which needs to be mounted far enough away to allow clearance for the handlebars on full lock. As a result, the Spada fairing offered very much better protection for the extremities of head and hands — areas which tend to be sacrificed for reasons of style or design compromise. There was also a bonus in that the lower side panel (leg shields), which were firmly fixed to the frame, could be removed individually with very little effort and without the need to disturb the main top fairing. This greatly simplified engine maintenance work.

All of the main mouldings were of fibreglass. The lower sections mounted close in to the frame, without the need for the bulky bracing tubes often needed to support large full fairings. Recessed cut-outs in their flanks allowed the cylinders to protrude into the cooling airstream and allowed very unrestricted access for top-end

1954 picture of the famed Guzzi wind tunnel: constructed originally for the factory's race efforts, it was later used to great advantage in the successful development of the streaming for the SP

work on the engine. Just above the cylinders were projecting, angled aerofoil sections, proved by the wind tunnel to increase the downthrust on the front wheel at speed, enhancing stability. The handlebar-mounted section overlapped the lower panels with a minimum clearance so that it presented an almost unbroken surface to the airflow, and a tinted, toughened perspex screen continued its smooth lines to direct the air current over the rider's head.

The lights were fitted into the top section, so that unlike a full fairing design, they would turn with the steering—an advantage in low-speed manoeuvres. The headlamp was a standard 170 mm diameter CEV unit, but the indicators were oblong, panel-mounted mouldings which continued the lines of the fairing with minimal intrusion into the airflow. Twin mirrors were also fitted to the top fairing which housed many of the 'extras' which set the Spada apart from its more mundane brothers in the Guzzi range.

Besides the usual speedometer and rev counter, there was a clock, mounted on the left,

and a matching voltmeter on the right. These instruments were all carried on a large, moulded rubber dash panel with the 'SP' logo, which also housed an array of warning lights and the central ignition switch. This dash panel was fitted to the contours of the fairing, as was a similar moulded rubber mat which fitted inside the base of the top section to protect the instruments, and the rider, from road filth which might otherwise be flung up through the joint between the sections.

The warning light cluster was split into two groups of four. The left-hand display consisted of a green light for the left turn signal, another green for neutral, a red generator warning light which went out when the engine was revved above tickover and the battery was charging, and a second red light to indicate low oil pressure. The right-hand display comprised a red light to indicate low oil level, a blue to show when the high beam was on, a green to show when the parking light was on, and a second green light from the right turn signal. The dash also had two more facilities not provided on the smaller V-twins—a switch for emergency flashers, and a trip meter which could be zeroed to record a chosen mileage.

The handlebar switches were also changed. The new design was characterized by various brightly coloured buttons that were aptly described by one journalist as looking 'as though they had escaped from a Monopoly set'. The left bar switches were arranged in two separate assemblies, and operated the lights and dip, the horn, flash and indicators. The right side carried just the starter and engine cut-out buttons.

One control that was not handlebar-mounted was the choke. This was in the usual Guzzi position, with a trigger mounted next to the left-hand carburettor, with a separate cable for each.

Apart from the fairing details, there was plenty

100SP marked Guzzi's first head-on challenge to the German BMW marque in the field of a luxury sports tourer

Showtime. The 1000SP debuted at the 1977 Milan Show and was hailed as one of two stars of the show; the other was Laverda's V6 endurance racer

6250 rpm, much greater than for the 850T3, but also a worthwhile improvement over the V1000 itself, which suffered from the energy-sapping disadvantages of the torque converter. In conjunction with its conventional 5-speed gearbox, the Spada's engine ensured the type of power well suited to its 'luxury touring' tag and motorway express role. A modification in the transmission was the adoption of a larger rubber bellows (boot) which covered a now heavier duty universal joint and linked the gearbox casing with the swinging arm.

The Spada's silencers were based on the upswept design used on the Le Mans, as opposed to the previous tourers' which had been horizontal. Unlike the Le Mans, however, they were in chrome.

More Le Mans parts were the wheels, of silver-painted cast alloy. The Spada featured the patented Moto Guzzi linked braking system with twin 300 mm front discs and a 242 mm rear, but with a couple of alterations. At the front, the brake calipers were mounted behind the fork legs, while at the rear a larger P9 caliper and a pressure relief valve were fitted in an attempt to cut down the rather-excessive wear rate which the linked system had induced on the rear disc. The suspension was standard Moto Guzzi equipment, but complemented by a friction-type steering damper.

The frame was virtually as before, but both stands had modifications designed to make life easier for the rider when parking the bike. The main priority in both cases had been to provide more effective operating arms, as these had proved a poor feature of the earlier V-twin models.

The tank design was clearly based on the T3, with a capacity of 24 litres, two manual fuel taps and a filler cap concealed under a hinged cover which could be released by the ignition key. But the seat was a totally different design from those used before. It must be said that it was not quite as luxurious as those fitted to either the T3 or the V1000, but it did offer the advantage of a

of evidence elsewhere of the care that had been taken to ensure that the Spada's general level of equipment was up to the standard of the Munich twins'. How much of an improvement its specifications were compared to those of the 850T3 can be seen at every level, starting, of course, in the engine department.

The V1000 engine with its bore and stroke of 88 × 78 mm and 9·2:1 pistons running in steel bores had a crankshaft power output of 71 bhp at 6500 rpm, and a useful torque rating of 8·6 kg/m at 5200 rpm. The Spada's power output to the back wheel was actually 54·91 bhp at

slightly lower height and more comfortable position for shorter riders. Under the seat, the rear mudguard carried a Le Mans II oblong tail light. The plastic front mudguard was of Le Mans pattern, but was actually somewhat longer.

Moto Guzzi's contemporary advertising brochure indicated their pride in their new creation, when it summed up the Spada thus; 'Moto Guzzi are proud to present a new standard of safety in motorcycle fairings. The new SP fairing was designed in the factory's famous wind tunnel, not just to be correct for the machine, but to be correct for the machine with rider mounted. This new design concept offers the rider not only protection from weather and outstanding

SP, a good blend of old and new in terms of engineering and style

streamlining, but with integral front spoilers the machine's front end is held more firmly on the road at high speeds. This new safer fairing combined with the Moto Guzzi unique integral brake system helps to make this new machine the world's safest, most beautiful and exciting motorcycle.'

Not just the wind tunnel, but a team of the factory's top test riders had been dedicated to proving the truth of these statements. Much of the early road testing was actually done on the autostrada system which links most of northern Italy, and during the summer of 1977, an intensive test programme was carried out prior to the Spada launch.

This debut took place in late November at the Milan Show, where a reputed 150,000 enthusiasts (a record number) swamped the various

stands on the exhibition's opening day. Two bikes stole the show that year. One was Laverda's V6 endurance racer, the other, Guzzi's new fully-faired tourer, then known simply as the 1000SP. The 23 November issue of *Motor Cycle News* reported; 'A more immediately available challenge to BMW comes from Guzzi with foot-change versions of their 1000 automatic. Sporting a normal five-speed box, instead of a torque converter, the new 1000SP has mag wheels and a nose fairing which gave Guzzi a splendid excuse to start up their old racing wind tunnel.'

It was to be a little while before the challenge to BMW would be felt on the world market, since immediately after the launch all production went to Italy. But by the following spring, quotas were being met which allowed the factory to start exports of the new model.

The first batch to reach Britain went on sale in early July 1978 at a cost of £2399. Colour options were either metallic gold or silver, and the Spada received a favourable reaction from both press and customers alike. Sales were excellent at the outset, and the bikes continued to sell well throughout the remainder of the year.

By this time, the Spada was in considerable demand at home, and in other export areas such as the important American market. In the States, the importer, the Premier Motor Corporation (an offshoot of the Berliner organization) was pushing the 1000SP as its main bike with full-page colour advertisements in magazines such as *Cycle* and

The factory even considered an 850 Le Mans SP; only one was actually constructed and never made it any further

103

Cycle World that proclaimed: 'Moto Guzzi—the internationally acclaimed touring machine . . . that out-performs ordinary bikes. . . .'

Despite the initial euphoria, however, the world's market for luxury tourers was inevitably limited and so the sales could not continue for very long at the first, high level. In Britain, the drop came in early 1979, and by the spring of that year sales had slowed to such an extent that the importers, Coburn & Hughes had built up a considerable excess stockpile of the Spada model. Faced with this situation, it was not long before they were looking for a way to move the bikes more quickly and release some of their capital investment.

The 1000SP powered Triking 3-wheeler, constructed by the Norwich company Triking Cars headed by Tony Divey (driving), at the MCC High Speed Trial Silverstone event, in October 1984

Enter the Spada Royale. This was a limited-edition model created by the British importers and designed to confer an aura of exclusivity that might attract the customer for whom this cachet was as important as the bike itself. Most noticeably, the Royale treatment consisted of a special paint finish in metallic cherry red and silver. This was done in the UK, by custom paint specialists, Dream Machine of Long Eaton in Nottingham. A practical addition to the specification was the fitting of a set of deluxe lockable panniers made by Sigma of Birmingham.

When the Royale was introduced, the basic Spada's price had gone down to £2299. But exclusivity commands an exclusive price, and so the Royale was tagged at an extra £500, at £2799. These rather clever tactics worked so well that demand for the Royale was high, and in its wake the basic Spada picked up too. By August 1979, supplies of the 100 Royales constructed were

running low and the standard model was in sufficient demand for its price to be increased to £2554.

The success of the Royale had convinced Coburn & Hughes that the exclusive model game was worth playing again, with the result that another special 'limited edition', the Black Prince, was introduced later on that year. As the name suggested, the bike was finished in black throughout, relieved only gold pin-striping on the tank, side panels and fairing, and offset by the silver-painted wheels, alloy cylinders and chrome exhausts.

The Black Prince proved to be another profitable sales venture, and one which helped the importers to achieve their target of running down the Spada stock completely in readiness for the imminent launch in early 1980 of a factory modified variant. This was the SP NT80, known more simply as the Spada NT.

In truth, the NT80 was hardly a new model. The original bike had simply gained new, more restrictive silencers, Nickasil bores in place of the steel liners, the V1000's more comfortably padded seat, and a few other very minor detail changes. New colours replaced the former gold or silver—metallic ice blue or metallic pale green. There was also none of the previous model's extensive use of matt black. Where this had been used on a panel in the middle of the tank, and again on the top fairing, the NT's base colour now covered the whole area. The only matt black parts remaining were in the recessed areas of the lower fairing surrounding the cylinder heads.

1000SP NT80. 'Operation NT' organized by the British importers Coburn & Hughes got the ball rolling in April 1980. Changes included silencers, seat and minor engine details

Once again, British importers Coburn & Hughes had conceived a very clever sales ploy, nicknamed 'Operation NT'. This was simply a way of selling the first batch of bikes to the dealer network and at the same time getting each of these dealers to have a demonstration model for the official launch. Operation NT saw 25 British Guzzi dealers (who were invoiced for their bikes), two of the importers' staff and two journalists arriving in person to collect the first 29 NTs from the factory in Italy—the idea being that they would then make a fast trans-European crossing together as a demonstration of the machines' touring capabilities. The members of the press, it was hoped, would report suitably on the affair, while the dealers would retain the machines as demonstrators.

Coburn & Hughes director Clew Hughes controlled the operation from the company's Beechcraft Baron six-seater aircraft, while another C & H employee went by road with a back-up van to the exercise. Six of the party (including the two journalists) were piloted by Clew Hughes himself from Luton airport via Cannes in the South of France. This trip was famous for producing a story which has since gone down as part of the motorcycle dealer's folklore, when one of the party (who had also incidentally contrived to forget his passport) was overcome by airsickness and was only deterred at the last minute from an emergency use of his crash helmet unforeseen by its makers, when a plastic bag was proffered by one of his fellow passengers!

Such minor mishaps apart, the whole British party finally reached the factory only to discover

1982 SP NT, with very smart red and white colour scheme

that the plant was on strike and the bikes were not yet ready. Fortunately, a skeleton workforce had remained, and were able to prepare the bikes with a delay of just one day. The next morning, 29 identical pale green NTs and their British riders assembled at the factory gates for their trip across Europe.

Tim Maton of Oxford Motorcycle Engineers was one of the riders and recalled that the bikes were not as trouble-free as no doubt Coburn & Hughes had hoped. Many of them were driven hard from the start, and with no proper running-in, several suffered from partial seizure problems. But they were pleasant to ride, and even when driven hard, the fuel consumption figures were 45 mpg—with 60 mpg easily attainable if speed was not essential.

Operation NT had taken place in April, and the new model went on sale in Britain in May at £2709. The NT was to continue with no changes except to price and paint finish until late 1983. Although in Britain Coburn & Hughes tried to reintroduce the limited edition idea with a model called the Mistral and fitted with panniers, this time the venture was a failure and the Mistral only lasted from February 1982 until May of that year. In any case, from the beginning of 1982, the factory had themselves been offering the Spada NT in a striking red and white paintwork which did much to improve its appearance as

Based on the T5, the 1000SPII made its public debut at the Milan Show in November 1983 and entered production early in 1984, greatly changed from the previous model

well as aiding its safety by increasing the machine's visibility to other road users. The price continued to rise, in Britain partly accounted for by the imposition of an 8 per cent 'car tax' on new motorcycles from March 1981. By the spring of 1983, the UK price was up to £3459.

In November 1983, the Milan Show was again the venue for the launch of a new Spada. This was called the SPII, and it really was significantly changed in many important areas. Its engine now featured the angular head and barrel finning seen on the California II and Le Mans III and 850T5 models. The improved cylinder head layout brought the power up to 67 bhp at 6700 rpm at the crankshaft, equivalent to 58·12 bhp at the rear wheel—although peak torque went down to 6·54 kg/m at 5750 rpm. But it was in the cycle parts that the major alterations had been made.

The machine's whole style and appearance was noticeably different. A 16 in. cast alloy front wheel replaced the old 18 in. fitting, and both wheels now had ten straight spokes instead of 12 cranked ones. Wider tyres, a 110/90 H16 front and 130/80 H18 rear, emphasized the ground-hugging attitude that this change conferred. The brake discs were now standardized to 270 mm diameter all round, and were drilled and plated which gave them a quite different appearance.

The basic frame remained as it had been when the Spada was introduced, but it was now dressed in many new parts. One fitting which was not altered was the fairing—a design which had proved again and again how effectively the development work had been done. But behind it was a new tank design with an increased 26-litre capacity. Also new were the seat and passenger grab rail, the mudguards and the side panels. And one small change broke with a Guzzi tradition when twin windtone horns replaced the previous type that had been on the larger Guzzi twins for almost 20 years. The finish was in red and black throughout, with red used on the tank, side panel and fairing, as well as the wheels. Black was used for the frame, lower forks, cylinder recesses in the fairing, and rocker covers.

Altogether the effect was striking, and these major changes to the Spada signalled the welcome news to admirers of the big Guzzi V-twins the world over that the fully-faired model still had a place in the company's future plans. Despite the demise of other models such as the V1000, G5 and the trusty T3, the Spada was to soldier on—an indication of the good sense of the factory in seeking to take on the prestigious luxury touring market.

8 | Middleweights for the masses

When Guzzi declared their intention to double the factory's production from its 1975 figures by the end of 1978, the management realized that there were several deficiencies in the model range which would have to be made up before they could hope to achieve this aim. Most noticeable of these was the yawning gap in between the current 125/250 two-strokes and the larger V-twin models. Although, in theory, this should have been filled by the 500 Falcone Nuovo single and the Benelli-designed four-cylinder 400GTS, the stark fact was that both of these had proved poor sellers.

If Guzzi were to make headway in this important market sector, it was obvious that a new machine was needed, and so De Tomaso instructed chief designer Lino Tonti to produce a middleweight V-twin that would capitalize on the factory's existing reputation for this engine configuration. The design had to be capable of mass-production, and it had to be suitable for adaptation to a range of alternative engine capacities.

The result was everything that De Tomaso could have wished, based on a 90-degree V-twin ohv four-stroke with shaft drive that closely followed the larger Guzzis. Emerging first as the V35/V50, Guzzi's new middleweight later spawned the larger V65 and a host of derivatives in standard, sports, custom and trail trim—making it the factory's most important and influential design of the 1970s.

Tonti began his design work during 1975, and

by the following spring, prototypes in both 350 and 500 cc forms were being road-tested after a successful series of trials on the bench. The target for the completion of the new bikes, now named V35 and V50, was the 1976 Cologne Show—held bi-annually in West Germany.

Guzzi correctly felt that the new middleweight V-twins, on which so much depended, demanded the top treatment. The factory had luckily chosen the major show of the year to launch their new bikes, with only Yamaha (XS250/360 twins) and Honda (CB125T pushrod twin) showing new models. This enabled Guzzi to grab headlines like, 'Cologne—Guzzis smell success'.

As De Tomaso had intended, the appearance of the two machines caused great interest both in Italy and abroad. The smaller version was an instant hit at home, for it offered Italian riders a unique opportunity to buy a shaft drive machine which fell into the low taxation category offered for under-350 machines. Overseas markets showed more enthusiasm for the larger version, since the V50 offered a promising alternative to Honda's brand new CX500.

But although these initial impressions indicated a great future for the new Guzzis, in truth, things behind the scenes were less rosy, with two serious threats to production. Both of these stemmed from the same cause—the limited manufacturing and assembly facilities at Mandello del Lario. At the end of 1976, the plant was almost at full stretch, and was completely unable to cope with the extra capacity needed for the V35/50. This led to very few bikes actually being built in 1977, which was when volume production of the two models should have started, and also meant that the manufacturing costs

1977 V50 from the first domestic production batch. Not sold outside Italy because of high costs before former Innocenti production facilities in Milan came on stream

were much greater than originally intended. As a result, the V50 cost so much that it was effectively ruled out of its planned role in export sales. The situation at Mandello was so grave that a contemporary report estimated the annual production capacity would be as low as 2,000 units using the existing facilities and assuming that Guzzi kept up their other commitments.

Although the situation looked desperate, De Tomaso had already seen and understood the problem. There were very good reasons not to monopolize the Mandello plant's spare capacity, for they could and did sell all the 850 and 1000 models which they could produce. And it was plainly silly to use any slack time in the assembly of different machines selling for half the price. The only answer was to find a new production line.

De Tomaso's net was so wide that he did not have to look very far for his solution. By mid-1978 it was clear that the new home for the V35 and V50 was to be the old Innocenti plant in south Milan, once the factory behind Lambretta that fuelled the scooter boom of the 1950s and 60s, and latterly the makers of the Innocenti version of the British Leyland Mini, and then their own, home-styled mini car.

Using his contacts within the American automobile industry, the Guzzi chief organized a large consignment of American machine tools with which to re-equip the lines for production of the V-twins. Conversion of the Innocenti factory got under way in the latter part of 1978, and by the beginning of 1979 things were starting to roll, with the promise both of meeting production quotas and of making a significant saving in unit cost. At last it looked as though both the Italian dealers and the various overseas importers could

Nearside view of early production V50; both the V50 (and V35) were smaller overall than most Japanese 250s

get their hands on the supplies that they wanted—and at the right price.

The world's press had already sampled the new middleweights during the previous year, even including reviews from countries which didn't receive any bikes. This included Britain, where the magazine *Which Bike?* voted the V50 top of a four-bike comparison test against the Yamaha XS500, the Morini 500 and the Honda CX500. *Which Bike?* concluded, 'So for the moment, Messrs Yamaha, Morini and, in particular Honda, can rest easy, for as far as this writer is concerned, the Moto Guzzi is the best of the bunch when it comes down to enthusiast motorcycling'—simply because the V50 was not available.

Early 1979, the improved V50II became available. Innocenti manufactured at last, Guzzi were able to begin proper export, at prices competitive with Honda's CX500 watercooled V-twin

Despite many such plaudits, however, neither the V35 nor the V50's chassis or engine offered anything particularly remarkable to account for the bikes' outstanding performance in comparison with their contemporaries. On the contrary, both relied entirely on the engineering traditions established by the larger Guzzi V-twins over the previous two decades, beginning with the first V7.

There were basically two things about the V35/50 design which made it such a strong contender in the middleweight stakes—the price (after 1979), and the incredibly low weight (particularly for a shaft drive bike) of a mere 303 lb (152 kg) dry. It was over 100 lb lighter than the tubby Honda V-twin and 80 lb less than Yamaha's less successful XS500 dohc parallel twin. Its size, too, matched its weight, and the little Guzzi was even smaller than many Japanese 250 cc of the era. This factor endeared it to smaller riders in particular.

A detailed look at the V35/50 proves just how clever the new middleweight design really was, and how it was able to acquire an almost instant niche in the market for Guzzi, both at home and abroad. The machines' success was built on several factors—the use of existing technology and advanced mass-production techniques resulted in price savings to Guzzi and customer alike, while the bikes themselves were attractively compact and had the very real advantage of an excellent power to weight ratio. Moto Guzzi could have turned this into the biggest selling Italian motorcycle of all time, but that they did not is ultimately due to three factors—marketing, quality control, and the general world recession from 1981 onwards. And only two of these were in Guzzi's power to control.

Marketing has never been a particularly strong point of the Italian motorcycle factories, which have characteristically proved either simply unwilling or unable even to approach the effectiveness of the Japanese organizations (or BMW). The inefficiency of the sales operation behind the V35 and V50 was to lend yet more evidence in support of this basic assertion, but even if Guzzi had pushed the machines more effectively, a spate of early failures was already indicating that the design was not as bullet-proof in service as the larger V-twins. These problems were by no means insurmountable, as Guzzi went on to prove, but the main factor which was outside their control was the general drop in motorcycle sales of the 1980s. This was an unfortunate fact of life that a mere motorcycle producer was largely unable to influence, since it stemmed from a world economic recession that no improvement in the quality of the product would affect. The recession took a similar toll from even the giants of the industry—witness the fate of Yamaha, who lost a reported £80 million in 1983 alone.

World factors apart, the little Guzzis had a good deal to recommend them apart from the eulogies of the press. Enthusiasts familiar with the

V50II engine. This photograph clearly shows the difference between the cylinder head/barrel design and that of the larger V-twins

'traditional' Guzzi V-twin would have no difficulty in recognizing these as smaller versions of their big brothers, starting from a very similar engine and running gear.

The engines had externally identical dimensions, but a bore and stroke of 66×50.6 mm for the V35 (74×57 mm for the V50) gave them capacities of 346·23 cc and 490·30 cc respectively. The V35's maximum crankshaft power rating was 33·6 bhp at 8100 rpm, while the larger engine produced 45 bhp at 7500 rpm. To take account of this, the primary drive ratios were different, with 1·846 on the 350 and 1·642 on the 500, and the helical gears in the final drive were also matched to the output, with 13/24 and 14/23 respectively.

Both engines had 10·8:1 compression ratios. Like the larger Guzzis, their pistons were offered in three sizes Class A at 66 000 to 66·006 mm (74·000 to 74·006), Class B at 66·006 to 66·012 mm (74·006 to 74·012), and Class C at 66·012 to 66·018 mm (74·012 to 74·018). The range of sizes enabled the pistons to be matched to the cylinders accurately, as on the bikes with chrome bores, although the bores were now Nicasil coated, rather than chromed.

The pistons were fitted with three rings, and an unusual feature of their construction was the use of concave crowns. This was a result of the cylinder head layout, which did not follow traditional Guzzi practice. Instead of the normal hemispherical combustion chamber and angled valves, the inside of the head was flat, with both valves parallel. Space for combustion was thus provided in the top of piston, rather than in the head. Although new to Guzzi, the system was well-tried, Heron heads, as they were called, having been applied on Jaguar cars and Morini V-twins, amongst others.

The valve sizes differed slightly between the two engines. The exhaust valves were identical at 27·6 mm diameter, but the inlet valves on the 350 were 30·6 mm instead of 32·6 mm on the 500. Twin coil springs were fitted to each valve, which ran in an iron guide retained in the head by a circlip. Although the inlet valve sizes were different, both bikes had identical carburettors— 24 mm square slide Dell'Orto VHBZs—and the inlet ports had inward facing manifolds which were connected to the carburettor by a rubber sleeve.

A distinctive feature of the new engine was the square finning of the cylinder heads, and this was matched by the angular rocker covers, carried on six Allen screws. The deep fins of the head casting carried two anti-resonance rubber blocks, similar to those fitted to many air-cooled two-strokes, to reduce fin ringing. Each cylinder head and barrel had two long and two short tie-bolts, by which they were retained to the crankcase.

The crankcase itself, unlike the larger V-twins,

V35II; a cross between the V50II and the series III models

was in two pieces, split horizontally and held together by ten studs of varying length. The crank carried two bolt-up steel conrods with 15 mm gudgeon pins running in bronze small-end bushes. Again, there were Class A (blue) and B (white) con rods which had to be matched to cranks with the same coding. The standard big-end diameter was between 34·987 and 34·999 mm, while the main bearings had a diameter of between 32·910 and 32·894 mm for the front (timing end) bearing, and from 34·988 to 40·008 mm for the rear (drive end) bearing.

The engine was lubricated in a similar fashion to the larger V-twins, with a lobe-type pump circulating the oil at a pressure of between 4·2 and 4·8 kg/cm². But a new feature was a different pattern of disposable oil filter housed in the sump. Unlike the earlier twins, it was possible for this to be replaced with the sump in place.

Transmission was similar to that on the bigger vees, but there were some important differences.

As on the larger machines, the clutch was housed inside the large ring gear for the electric starter. But unlike them, the clutch itself was a true single-plate diaphragm type, consisting of the friction plate, pressure cap, pressure plate and diaphragm spring. The spring had a design load capacity of 160 kg (350 lb) when compressed to 4 mm.

The five-speed constant mesh gearbox had frontal engagement, with a left-hand gearchange lever, and the internal ratios were identical on both the V35 and the V50—but the gears themselves were straight-cut, rather than helical as on the larger twins. Final drive was by a fairly traditional Guzzi shaft arrangement but the rear universal joint carried a long extension as on the

V50III. Points ignition replaced the previous Bosch electronic ignition. Other changes included higher engine tune, different silencers and lots more

Engine of the V35II tested by the author in *Motorcycle Enthusiast* **during 1984**

V1000, and was protected by a new type of rubber boot (gaiter).

The gearbox had the provision for installation of an optional kickstarter, swinging out on the right-hand side, but the normal method of starting was electric, with a Bosch DG 12-volt starter motor rated at 0·7 hp.

The battery was not especially large at 12-volt 20-amp hour, and an optional 32-amp hour one was available if starting took too great a toll. The alternator, a Bosch G1(R) 14V 20 A21 was well able to cope. Bosch also provided the regulator and rectifier, as well as the electronic ignition system, which consisted of two magnetic pick-up units and two transducers. Completing the electrical equipment was the 170 mm CEV headlight with its 12-volt 40/45 watt bulb, a twin-bulb rear light, black indicators, single Belli horn, and a panel of four warning lights on the instrument panel. The handlebar switchgear was the same garish 'Monopoly set' found on the Spada and Le Mans.

The middleweight vees had a double-cradle frame which followed the usual Guzzi lines by having detachable bottom tubes that would allow the engine to be dropped out from below with ease. In fact, the whole drive train—engine, gearbox, drive shaft and rear wheel—together with the exhaust system, could be detached from the frame, forks and front wheel to give truly amazing accessibility.

The swinging arm was in cast alloy, pivoting on the rear of the gearbox casing, and it was suspended from the frame by three-way or five-way adjustable Sebac suspension units with exposed chrome springs. Front forks were of Guzzi's own manufacture and had 35 mm stanchions and an effective travel of 125 mm. As on the rest of the range, the forks had sealed internal damper units, made by Lispa. The steering head bearings were cup and cone, each carrying 25 steel balls.

At the time of the models' introduction, cast alloy wheels were much in vogue, so these were a standard fitting. The pattern adopted by Guzzi had 12 spokes and a silver painted finish. Both wheels were 18 in. in diameter, and carried the superb Guzzi linked braking system. The discs were of smaller size than usual (twin 260 mm at the front and a single 235 mm rear) to suit the machines' lighter weight, and had smaller Brembo calipers and square pads.

The front calipers were mounted on lugs forward of the fork legs, and the left front brake and rear caliper were operated by the master cylinder next to the rear brake pedal. The right front brake was operated by a master cylinder mounted at the front of the top frame tube, between the cheeks of the fuel tank. This was in turn actuated by a short cable running from the handlebar lever itself. Among the Guzzi range, this system was unique to the V35 and V50, but it had been used earlier by BMW and Kawasaki, and the theoretical advantage of the added complication was supposed to be that the vulnerable master cylinder was not exposed to damage.

Both models shared the same colour schemes, the choice being between red or metallic blue/grey. These colours were used on the tank, plastic side panels, mudguards and headlamp brackets, while the frame, headlamp shell and many minor parts were painted black. Like the wheels, the fork bottoms and swinging arm were painted silver, and the complete exhaust system was chrome-plated. As well as the body colour, the tank also carried a matt black centre panel like the Le Mans, running from front to rear all the way across the flat top of the tank.

When the new Innocenti factory production lines came onto stream in early 1979, manufacture of both the V35 and V50 was transferred completely to their new home in the industrial area of Milan. And at the same time, several design changes were incorporated into both

models, with the larger bike being known from then on as the V50II.

The original design had an oil capacity of 2·25 litres. This was now increased to 2·5 litres by making the finned sump casting deeper—this also required a different type of gasket. In place of the polished alloy outer timing cover, both bikes now had a black plastic moulding, but the rocker covers were polished.

All the other changes were made on the 500 only, and were virtually entirely cosmetic rather than mechanical. The only functional change was to the front brake discs which were of a different pattern although still the same size. The headlamp received a chrome-plated rim and the headlamp shell was now held by two Allen bolts instead of the hexagon bolts used before. The black CEV indicators were changed for Larghi chrome items and these gained matching

Sporty looks but hardly any improvement in performance, the V35 Imola was launched in 1979

V40 Imola, a special model almost certainly for the French market to combat that country's Value Added Tax regulations. Was it actually a 350?

at 27·6 mm for the inlet and 26·6 mm for the exhaust. The USA V50 had side reflectors fitted to its CEV indicators, a sealed beam headlamp and other minor modifications to comply with American legislation. The Dutch market V50 had modified exhaust pipes, but these were fitted for no readily apparent reason.

The British importers were able to accept the standard Italian-market V50II, with the only alterations being a mile-per-hour speedometer and headlamp that dipped on the correct side (although there were certainly some on which the headlamp was not changed). When imports to the British Isles began in April 1979, the model cost £1475, which dropped to £1299 in August that year when the new bike was selling at its peak. The reason for the reduction was the high level of confidence induced by a record number of Guzzi sales in Britain, mainly due to the initial sales success of the middleweight V-twin.

Everything seemed to be rolling smoothly, on the surface, at least, with the popular press giving the thumbs up to the new Guzzi in no uncertain terms. A typical headline was *Motor Cycle News*' comment, 'Best handling bike I've ever ridden'. In fact, buoyed up by such exuberance, the importers Coburn & Hughes were to sell over 2000 V50s in that first year, a higher figure than that for all the other Guzzis *and* Ducatis which they imported put together.

But behind the scenes, many of the dealers (and customers) were far from happy, for the V50 was generating a large number of claims under warranty. The only good thing that could be said about these was that they were restricted to a small number of different complaints, but each of the faults was annoyingly common. These included failure of the flanges and oil seals in the final drive, failure of the fork oil seals, trouble with the ignition switch, and the poor finish. The standard of finish in particular could be appalling, with whole flakes of paint falling off the plastic side panels (self-coloured in red!)

None of these panels appeared to be prepared

chrome brackets, one-piece at the front and fixed to the bottom yoke. The yoke itself was now polished alloy rather than black.

The paintwork on the V50II was more elaborate, with thin lining in orange and yellow running on either side of the fuel tank and on the side panels above and below the badges. The 'V50' logo on the side panels now incorporated a 'II'.

There were also a number of modifications designed for individual export markets. The German V35 saw the most, with the carburettors reduced in size to 20 mm and revised main jet and needle sizes. There were matching smaller inlet manifolds and inlet ports, and smaller valves

Customer cruiser. Guzzi's answer to the growing popularity of the American custom craze which swept Italy during 1982

for painting in any way, and when they flexed, the paint would lose all adhesion on the shiny surface. All of these annoyances witnessed a somewhat different story from the rave reviews of the motorcycle journalists, for while there was no doubt that the machine was a joy to ride, living with an early V50II was not such an endearing experience.

By mid-1980, these problems had reached the point where sales were beginning to be affected. To counter the drop, and update the bike generally, a new version of the model was introduced later in the year. Known as the V50III, this did

have a much better level of finish, both in terms of the paintwork and plating. The front mudguard which had previously been steel, was replaced by a plastic one although some late V50IIs also had this fitted. A new headlamp with a quartz bulb was fitted, and the direction indicators were changed again—this time to black, oblong ones with matching black stems. The front indicator mounting was a one-piece affair incorporating a grille and Moto Guzzi emblem, as well as the headlamp brackets, which made it a more costly item to replace in the event of an accident.

The front master cylinder was moved up from under the tank to the conventional place on the handlebar adjacent to the lever, which now operated it directly. The front brake discs were changed again, to a drilled type (as were some late V50IIs), and the calipers were relocated behind the fork legs. The area formerly occupied by the master cylinder reservoir was now taken up by a modified cover for the fuel filler cap. On the V50II, this was a simple hinged plastic flap, but now the cover was metal and hid a chrome filler cap.

The saddle and silencers were also changed, and the machine was given a new choice of colours—red or brown. The matt black upper panel on the tank was dispensed with, and the rear light was finished integrally with the plastic mudguard. Together these changes contributed to a considerable change in the machine's appearance, reflected in its adoption of new 'V50III' decals.

But it was not just a case of mutton dressed as lamb, for there were mechanical changes as significant as any of this window dressing. Although the compression ratio remained unaltered, the power went up to 47 bhp at 7500 rpm, achieved by increasing the inlet and exhaust valve diameters to 34 and 30 mm respectively. The carburation was also uprated by increasing the choke size to 28 mm, using round slide PHBH BS/BD instruments. To take full advantage of the freer breathing, larger diameter inlet manifolds and exhaust pipes were fitted. In the transmission, the gear selectors and gears themselves were modified.

The V50 had suffered from an annoying flat spot which might have been put down to carburation, but was in fact a product of the Bosch

Below **Smaller engined custom, the V35C. Where were the Hell's Angels?**

Right **Popular V65 was made in** *normale* **and SP** (*speciale*) **versions. Can you spot the differences?**

electronic ignition system. So a very significant alteration was the fitting of twin Dansi contact breakers and condensers. Some would argue that cost was the sole reason for this change but whatever the case the flat spot was cured— instead the points heel wore excessively causing a loss in performance and the need for constant adjustment.

The various modifications showed up immediately on the road, as a much more lively performance and, in my opinion, improved handling as

well. The maximum speed had risen from a shade over the magic 'ton' to a genuine 105 mph, but even more importantly, and more usefully, the level of acceleration was also improved.

In line with the improvements to the V50, the V35 had also been updated (but only once) when a new version, the V35II, was first shown on the Guzzi stand at the Milan Show in November 1979. Quite simply, it was the V50II chassis around a V35 engine with the performance improvements and new silencers of the V50III. It had the V50III type of seat, and the black plastic timing cover and points ignition. The front drilled brake discs were V50III and the calipers were similarly fitted behind the forks. The carburettors were enlarged to 26 mm instead of 24 mm, and

V35TT; this name had no connection with the Isle of Man, but actually stood for *tutto terreno* **(all terrain) and was available in both 350 and 650 engine sizes**

larger inlet manifolds and exhausts were used, although no steps had been taken to alter the valve diameters to correspond.

The V35II's colour schemes were red (like the V50) or silver and from early 1982 in metallic lime green. Like the V50III, there was no matt black on the tank, but the striping followed the lines of the original V35.

When testing a V35II in the autumn of 1984, I found it slightly quicker than the original model, with a top speed of 93 mph (2 mph up on the V35), and although it was perhaps no faster than many a 'touring' Japanese 250 twin, it nevertheless offered an almost ideal lightweight sports/tourer for the mature rider who had no need for an excess of power. I also found that the small

Guzzi had a clunk-free gearchange with which first gear could be engaged noiselessly every time—even from cold.

Areas which did not earn praise included the prop stand, which, with an action like a mousetrap, proved difficult to use—particularly because the lack of an extension arm made it perilously easy to contact the hot exhaust pipe when operating the stand. Equally poor were the access to the nearside carburettor (except for basic adjustment), the vulnerable indicators and

The V65TT offered an excellent power to weight ratio and it utilized the same running gear and chassis as the 350 version

mountings, and the design of the rear mudguard location, which allowed both the guard itself and the indicator support to be damaged in the event of the bike being dropped. Another poor feature was the weak design of the throttle mounting on the handlebar, which comprised a single miniature grub screw that was simply inadequate to anchor a plastic component onto the metal bar.

In contrast to the fault-finding, I praised the V35II's superb rideability. What power there was could be used to the full in complete safety, with the rider being able to drive the bike as hard as required on rough or smooth road surfaces. Combined with the linked braking system, the smoothness of the engine (noticeably better than the V50) and the light weight, these qualities made it a uniquely forgiving bike. I felt it was the one machine which could be ridden in city traffic or twisty country lanes with the same level of

satisfaction. The only thing which would let it down was its lack of speed if asked to go motorway cruising.

But the V35II never set out to be a performance bike. If that was what you wanted, then Guzzi had not been standing still with sporting versions of the design, either. The first of these based on the middleweight V was the V35 Imola, which made its appearance (like the V35II) at the 1979 Milan Show.

Essentially, the Imola looked much more sporting than it really was. The engine even used the same compression ratio and the same carburettors as the standard V35II. The factory quoted an extra 1 bhp, while the peak revs rose

Named after its birthplace, the Lario was Guzzi's first 4-valve per cylinder production V-twin, entering the market place in early 1984

to 8200 rpm. This was a result solely of larger valves—a 30·5 mm inlet and 27·5 mm exhaust—because everything else was standard.

Most of the running gear was shared with the V35II, but the sports bike gained a neat bikini fairing, clip-ons, rearsets, a new dualseat with a racing-style tailpiece, upswept silencers and the indicators from the V50III. Handling was assisted by air suspension front and rear, the latter units now being exclusively of Paioli manufacture. The tank capacity was increased to 16 litres and the finish was an eyecatching Italian racing red for the fairing, tank (with a black base and top), mudguards, side panels, fork bottoms and seat tail section. There were no badges or lining, simply a gold 'Moto Guzzi eagle' transfer on the front of the fairing and each side of the tank, and 'V35 Imola' on the side panels.

Credit must be given to the stylist who, with the minimum of outlay, transformed the pack-

age from a humble tourer to a lithe sportster—even though in this case the exciting looks did not actually mean much in the way of increased performance except that generated by the revised riding position and the streamlining. With the rider flat on the tank and tucked in behind the fairing, the maximum speed rose to 99 mph.

At the Bologna Show in 1980, Moto Guzzi did the obvious thing and introduced the V50 Monza, a larger version of the Imola. This had a standard V50III engine but with different primary gear ratio, housed in the Imola cycle parts. The only differences between the two apart from the engine size and primary gearing were the side panel transfers and the colour scheme, with metallic grey/blue as an option to the red.

The Lario was produced in both five hundred—the V50 Monza II . . .

Unlike the V35 Imola, the V50 Monza *was* imported into Britain, and the first deliveries arrived in February 1981 at a price of £1699, some £200 more than the standard V50III. Even so, the Monza soon found a ready market, although like the later version of the V50, it never approached the heady sales figures of 1979.

When *Motorcycling* tested the Monza, they recorded a maximum speed of 105·35 mph prone and fuel consumption figures of 58 mpg overall. Interestingly, their tester discovered that the Monza was actually—'far more at home over the bumps and potholes along the country lanes' than the Le Mans II he had just tested! But, 'like most Guzzis there is more noise from the induction system where the carbs make that chuff-chuff-chuffer-chuff-chuff sound so distinctive of the V-twin motor at low revs'.

The Milan Show held in November 1981 heralded a fresh Guzzi attack on the middle-weight market with a larger engine and full range of so-called US Custom-style machines. The new engine followed its smaller brothers in layout, even though both the bore and stroke—80 and 64 mm—were different from the V50. These dimensions gave a capacity of 643·4 cc, and except for this modification and the adoption of larger Dell'Orto PHBH 30 BD/BS carburettors, everything else was close to V50III specification.

Three versions of the V65 were shown at Milan—the Normale, Speciale (SP), and Custom. The first two were essentially V50IIIs with the larger engine, although the Speciale included a Spada-type three-piece fairing.

The Custom (also shown in 350 and 500 forms) was quite different. There were clear reasons why Guzzi should favour the introduction of a laid-back style version, for not only had Honda already introduced a CX500 Custom, but the US Custom style was also becoming extremely popular on the Italian home market, where, following

. . . and three-fifty V35 Imola II form

hard on the heels of the fashionable dirt bike boom, at the start of the 1980s, Italian riders had taken to cruising the streets on bikes that were more in keeping with LA than Bologna.

Guzzi's engineers followed Honda's lead very closely with a bike which looked superficially very similar to the CX500 Custom. All three capacity classes enjoyed the same looks, which extended from the 15-litre peanut tank back to the chrome mudguards and 16 in. rear tyre. Again, like their Japanese counterparts, Guzzi were building on much of the original bike and using completely standard engines.

1984 brochure depicting the V65TT. The factory did not produce a serious off-road racing version of this machine

The only really purpose-built items were the tank, king and queen saddle, chrome grab rail, chrome mudguards, ape hanger bars, side panels, and of course the fat 16 in. cast wheel and matching 130/90H16 Pirelli MT28 tyre fitted at the rear. The frame and forks, linked brakes and electrics were stock Guzzi, and even though the rear light and headlamp brackets were from the 850T3, rather than the middleweight range, the kicked-up silencers were from the Imola/Monza.

The Custom offered two colour options— either red, with black and gold lining, or metallic steel blue/grey with blue and black lining. But as much of the bike's finish was in chrome plate, the main colour was only applied to the tank and side panels.

The other 650s, the Normale and Speciale, had a choice of three colours—red, light metallic green (as on the Spada NT) and metallic steel grey. As on the V35/50 the main colour extended to the mudguards and also over the seat frame which extended around the seat pan from the pillion rider's section to the back. On the Speciale, the body colour was also employed all over the fairing, which had a tinted screen as on the other faired Guzzis.

Despite these new models, several of Guzzi's traditional markets did not respond in the way that the factory had hoped. In the USA, the Premier Motor Co was winding down its operation—to such an extent that Moto Guzzi themselves set up their own import company, called Guzzi USA, during 1983. Before that, very few Guzzi machines of any type were imported after 1980, and this hit the new middleweights hard. In Britain, the Guzzi importers since 1975, Coburn & Hughes, also imported very few bikes during 1982/83, but in early 1984 responded to pressures from Guzzi, their dealers and the press by importing a batch of 300 Guzzis, mainly 650s, but with some V35IIs and some of the larger V-twins making up the consignment.

The main interest was with the V65 Normale

and Speciale (called the SP in Britain) and a limited number of V65 Customs. The prices of these were £2299 for the V65, £2399 for the SP and £2529 for the Custom. Unfortunately for the importers, relatively few of these (reputed to be 67) were sold—and in desperation, Coburn & Hughes did a deal with the West German Guzzi importer in the autumn of 1984, as a result of which all the unsold bikes were shipped to Germany. Although no reason was given, this was in fact why Coburn & Hughes lost the importation rights for Guzzi in Britain, ending a partnership which had lasted for almost a decade and

seen a record number of Guzzis sold in the UK, estimated at around some 13,000 units.

Even before the termination of Coburn & Hughes' contract, other British companies had been looking at the Guzzi range. One, Motomecca of Clapham in London, had actually already started to bring in much of the range, albeit in small numbers, and were therefore in a position to take full advantage of the new models launched at the 1983 Milan Show—in particular an entirely new name—the Lario, the sporting version of the V65. Also shown at Milan were the Imola II and Monza II. All of these newcomers had four-valve cylinder heads and razor-sharp styling.

Not only did Milan offer these exciting sportsters but Guzzi also launched a pair of brand new off-road style models, known as the TTs. The TT name had no connection with the Isle of Man races, but actually stood of the Tutto Terreno (all terrain). In 350 and 650 versions, both TTs were identical except for the engine capacities, and the up-to-the-minute enduro styling with which they were endowed featured everything that would fulfil a road rider's dream of owning a pukka enduro bike, but without the hassle of a fire-breathing, noisy, maintenance-demanding machine that the real competition bike represents.

Add to the bikes' looks the civility and practicality of the middleweight Guzzi V-twin, and the factory had come up with a pair of machines certain to command attention, following the showing of a prototype—the V50TS at Milan in 1981. Like the Custom models, there was no change in engine specification from their standard brothers, but cosmetically the TTs were strikingly different. Topped off by a motocross-style 14-litre tank, the layout was extremely neat with flowing lines that continued through the side panels, and rear seat/mudguard section. The seat covering itself was a fashionable red with 'TT' emblazoned in blue and a peak at the front which extended up over the rear of the tank. The

1984 V65C Custom had screen panniers, king and queen seat and crashbars as standard equipment

switchgear was unchanged, as was the matching rev counter and speedometer. Only the prop stand was fitted, but a couple of useful additions were the large rubber mudflap which extended down to hide the timing cover at the base of the front mudguard, and the rubber gaiters on the Marzocchi front forks.

At the front, the enduro-style square head-lamp had a cowling with a red number-plate at the top and a series of air grilles below. This carried the front indicators, which were in black plastic and flexibly mounted on rubber stalks. The tail section, which doubled as part of the rear mudguard, also helped to support the rear light, indicators and a practical black luggage carrier. A nylon, unbreakable motocross front mudguard was colour-matched to the tank, side panels, tail section and front cowl in either white or steel grey.

The rest of the machine was equally colourful. The frame, the bodies of the Marzocchi Strada air assisted rear suspension units, the fork bottoms and yokes of the long-travel leading-axle

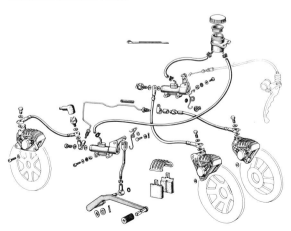

Guzzi patented linked brake system for the V35, 50 and 65 series. Virtually the same as that used on the bigger machines since the 750S3

38 mm Marzocchi front forks were all finished in red. The wheel hubs, complete exhaust system, braced handlebars, rear suspension springs, torque arm, levers and pedals were all finished in black. Instead of the usual polished rocker covers, these were now also in black, but the rest of the engine, the swinging arm and rear drive box retained their silver finish.

Both hubs were laced to Spanish Akront alloy rims, which usefully did not feature water-trapping wells. These were shod with a 3.00×21 in. front and 4.00×18 in. rear Pirelli MT enduro-pattern tyre. Front and rear brakes relied on a single Brembo caliper and 260 mm drilled disc—but unusually for a Guzzi V-twin, these were not linked.

The exhaust system is worth examining in detail. An almost standard pair of exhaust pipes fed from either side into a massive collector box which was two-thirds of the width of the engine unit. The collector was tucked in behind the finned sump, as close as possible to the crankcase. Even so, it, the sump and the sump shield without doubt limited the use of either TT model to only the most delicate of off-road use—go 'rock bashing' or 'berm burning' at your peril. From the collector box, a single pipe passed straight up behind the right-hand rear suspension leg to exit just to its rear into a silencer whose tailpipe extended neatly out just under the indicator on the same side of the machine.

If there were many at Milan whose eye was caught by the new off-roaders, even more were attracted to the three sportsters, which shared a common styling package. The Imola II, Monza II and Lario all had an 18-litre tank, side panels and tail section which blended in with each other, although in my opinion the styling was less effective than on the TT models. Somehow, the rear tail had just too much of a flip up tip, which made it a less than happy conclusion to the lines.

Technically, the most interest in the new designs was centred on their cylinder heads—

four-valve for the first time on a production Moto Guzzi. As before, the middleweight twins still used the Heron combustion chamber with parallel valves and recessed pistons, but now the valves were paired, using two smaller diameter valves in place of each larger one on the earlier models.

Like other Guzzi sportsters, much attention had been given to wind tunnel testing, and obviously the lessons learned from (and incorporated in) the 850 Le Mans III played in important part in the newcomers' streamlining. Although vestigial, the small top fairing and separate aerofoils were mounted in such a way that they deflected the air stream away from the rider, under the fuel tank and over the cylinder heads.

The front mudguard featured a built-in fork brace, for Guzzi had by then learned from other models with plain plastic guards that without bracing, the forks were liable to twist under heavy braking—impairing both the handling and the roadholding. The forks themselves were still Guzzi's own air-assisted units, but the fork bottoms were modified so that the axle was now actually slightly trailing. The rear suspension units were again by Paioli, a pair of gas shock absorbers.

Following the contemporary trends, both wheels were 16 in. fitted with 100/90 H16 front and 120/90 H16 rear Pirelli tyres. The brakes used three 270 mm drilled discs, and the front calipers were mounted behind the fork legs.

The rider's view of the bike was dominated by the instrument layout, which centred on a massive 100 mm diameter white-faced Veglia racing

V35 power unit and final drive assembly

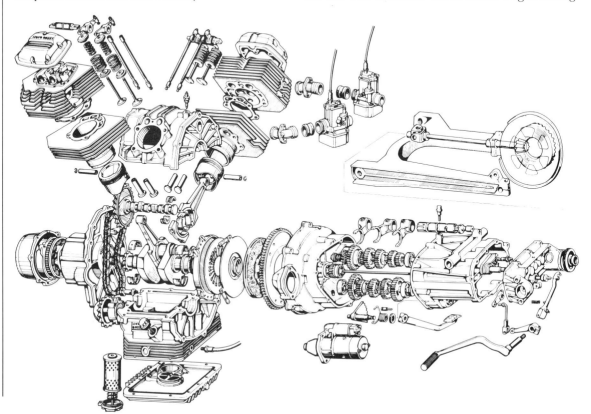

tachometer, with a smaller speedometer and matching voltmeter. After the pattern set by several of the larger twins—notably the Spada and Le Mans—the instruments were housed in a thick moulded rubber console, which also held the row of warning lights and the ignition switch.

All three models were in the same choice of colours—red or silver. The fairing, tank, seat fairing, fork bottoms, mudguards and bellypan were all colour matched, and although the main frame was painted black, the detachable lower rails were finished in red—as were the wheels, even though the outer rims were polished alloy. The cast alloy swinging arm was still painted silver—a treatment which was extended to the bulk of the engine, too. The latter move was an attempt to stop discoloration through corrosion of the alloy—a problem well known to British owners. The exhaust system was in a glossy black chrome finish, and from my experience of testing a V65 Lario , still suffered from the bane of that particular treatment—premature rust—as in this case oxidation had started in at the clamps and silencer weld seams. Later models, however, had a (longer lasting?) black chrome finish.

Judging by the Lario which I rode, the adoption of the four-valve heads was, in the final analysis, probably as much due to the demands of the marketing men as of the engineers, for there was no drastic improvement in the performance, although the exercise was certainly worthwhile. It was not so much simply that the new heads offered better breathing at high rpm, but also a useful amount of extra mid-range power that made the four-valve Guzzi noticeably different

from its predecessors. For the record, the Lario had a crankshaft power output of 60 bhp at 7800 rpm which compared with 50 bhp at the same revs for the four-valve 500, and 40 bhp at 8800 rpm for the V35 Imola II.

What impressed me most about the bike was its cobby, purposeful stance, and the excellent riding position in which rider and machine blended so well—even though a lighter clutch action would have been appreciated! I was left with the feeling that with the V65 Lario's sharp racy lines, good power to weight ratio and definitive sportster riding position, here, perhaps, was Guzzi's best sports machine of the 1980s—and a bike which could win many friends for the marque.

There had never been any doubt about the essential rightness of the Guzzi middleweights' frame and engine design, but for too long, the models had been dogged by minor faults that made living with them less of a pleasure than it should have been. General problems included frequent head gasket failure, and it was found that the valve adjustment was critical, for inattention would cause the exhaust valves to burn out. The carburettor connecting rubbers would perish and leak, and on the Monza and Imola, the carburettor balance was also difficult to maintain. And on all models, the rear bevel flange was too soft, so that the Teflon oil seal would actually wear the metal of the flange! Guzzi took far too long to tackle these problems, with the result that a model which started with a brilliant future received a tarnished reputation from which it never managed totally to recover.

9 | Badge engineering— mini twins

One of the first results of the acquisition of Moto Guzzi by the De Tomaso group was that the 250 Benelli 2C two-stroke twin underwent a change of identity. The new Moto Guzzi 250 that went on sale shortly after the take-over was virtually a straight example of badge engineering— certainly the engine unit, frame, forks and wheels were pure Benelli 2C. But there were styling changes aimed clearly at selling the little 'stroker to a more up-market clientele than would have been possible under the Benelli name.

With a new tank shape, reminiscent of the big twins, and better detail finish, the little Benelli became the Moto Guzzi 250TS—first sold in 1974 exclusively for the Italian home market. But before the end of the year, the 'new' Guzzi two-stroke had also been despatched to a few of the factory's overseas markets, including a handful sent to the then British importers, Barrett's of Redhill.

Although a relatively modern design (for 1972), the Benelli 2C had two glaring faults for anything other than the domestic market—weak, 6-volt electrics and a reliance on petroil mixing in the tank rather than a more convenient oil pump lubrication system. (In Italy petroil is available at filling stations from pumps, the oil percentage is simply dialled in.) Together, these limited its appeal to a much narrower section of potential customers than its good points—performance, handling and looks—merited.

The heart of the bike was a simple piston-port two-stroke twin with an actual capacity of

231·4 cc from a bore and stroke of 54 × 47 mm. Carburation was by a pair of square-slide Dell'-Orto 25VHBs. Early Benelli engines had cast-iron barrels, but the later 2C which was adopted by Moto Guzzi switched to alloy cylinders with chrome bores. Although the factory handbook quoted an optimistic 32 bhp at 7000 rpm, the true figures were 24·5 bhp at 7570 rpm—not so outstanding but nonetheless respectable.

The pistons used in the alloy barrels were made by Asso. They gave a 9·75:1 compression ratio and were fitted with two cast-iron rings and 18 mm gudgeon pins. The same pistons were also later to be used in the 125 Turismo single which shared the same bore size as the 250TS. It was this machine with which De Tomaso

A supposedly up-market version of the Benelli 250 2C, the Guzzi 250 2T first appeared in prototype form early in 1973 shortly after De Tomaso had acquired the Mandello del Lario factory

forged a brief link with the British Triumph factory at Meriden, when the 125 was assembled and sold in the UK as the Co-Uno (Cooperative One). Although it is not widely known, the 125 Turismo also used a con-rod assembly which was identical to the 250 engine's, with the same big-end and small-end caged roller bearings. This fact is particularly useful to anyone owning or contemplating rebuilding a 250TS (or Benelli 2C) because neither model's factory parts book listed separate con-rod kits, only complete crankshaft assemblies being available for the twins. The four-bearing built-up crankshaft itself owed much to Japanese constructional practice, as did the horizontally-split crankcases.

The gearbox had five speeds with a left-foot change and wet multiplate clutch. This had five steel plates and five identical friction plates, plus one additional friction plate of a different pattern which fitted behind them. The kickstarter was on the right.

Left **231·4 cc two-stroke twin with piston port induction offered excellent acceleration and general performance, but suffered from feeble 6-volt electrics and petrol/oil lubrication**

Below right **Similar to the winner of the 1974 Italian National Hillclimb championship, this Italian Formula 3 road racer was constructed in 1975 from a Guzzi two-stroke twin by REC in Genoa. Watercooled, it ran 46 bhp at 11,500 rpm**

Below **250TS on the Guzzi stand at the Paris Show, October 1973**

This engine unit was housed in a full duplex cradle frame, with 32 mm stanchion Marzocchi front forks and five-way adjustable Marzocchi rear suspension units. Braking was by Grimeca drums with a double-sided 180 mm single leading shoe at the front, and a single-sided 158 mm rear brake. These were laced into 18 in. chrome-plated rims using silver painted spokes.

Ignition and lighting were provided by Dansi, using a similar system to that which was employed on the Italian-made 175/250 Harley-Davidson (Aermacchi) two-strokes. But where Harley were wise enough to specify a 12-volt system, Benelli—and, of course, Moto Guzzi—were not. The Dansi system was basically a conventional flywheel magneto housing both ignition and lighting coils, with a pick-up for the electronic ignition mounted on the stator plate

so that when the flywheel was fitted it ran inside the pick-up leaving an air-gap of between 0·3 and 0·4 mm. This pick-up sensed the position of the flywheel and triggered the spark via an electronic 'black box' with five terminals (the ignition module), located under the seat, and twin ignition coils under the tank. Neither the ignition nor the main lights drew their power from the battery, a Varta 6V 9AH, which served only to store power for the secondary lights, horn and flashing indicators.

In all these details, the Benelli 2C and Moto Guzzi 250TS were identical. But it was the latter's style and appearance which separated it from the essentially mundane-looking Benelli. The Guzzi sported a larger, more bulbous 14-litre tank, together with a completely different seat and side panels which adopted the 'house style'

of the larger V-twins. Square-section chrome mudguards replaced the smaller, rounded stainless steel ones on the 2C, and the square CEV rear light from the 850T/T3 took the place of the Benelli's round one. Other new electrical specifications were a definite improvement over the originals, with 6-volt versions of the V-twins' 170 mm chrome CEV headlamp, Aprilia indicators and handlebar switchgear all helping to make the best of the limited power available. Early bikes had a pair of Silentium silencers which had a slashed end to a detachable cone at the rear. This was quickly changed to a more rounded version which improved the look of the machine.

Paintwork was all in metallic colours, with a choice of either lime green, kingfisher blue or a golden brown. The tank carried a metal 'Moto Guzzi' badge with a double gold strip on either side, no matter what the basic colour. The side

panels also carried this gold trim under a 250TS badge and 'Elettronica' transfer.

Looks apart, the little Guzzi had a lot going for it to outweigh the inconvenience of its electrical and lubrication systems. With a dry weight of 143 kg (317 lb) its performance was excellent—when Motorcycle News tested a TS in July 1975, they found it the quickest accelerating contemporary 250, with a standing quarter figure of 15·22 seconds and a maximum speed of 88·24 mph. But its outstanding feature was its superb handling, which meant that even though it might seem underpowered by Japanese quarter-litre roadster standards, the Italian twin could usually hold its own by dint of its lighter

Styled on similar lines to the Guzzi GTS 350/400 four-cylinder four-strokes of the period, the 250TS gained new forks, disc front brake and instrument console at the end of 1975

weight and greater bend-swinging ability.

This trait was to lead to its use as a successful racer in both production classes and Italian F3 events. But it also made the basis of a great bike for sprinting, winning the 1974 Italian National Hillclimb Championships with a special version built by the Genovese firm REC. Named for Romei and Cipriani, respectively the designer and rider, the REC also won the Italian Junior championships in that year. In 1975, a water-cooled version was constructed, and replicas of this machine went on general sale. Its specifications included enlarging the capacity nearer to 250 cc, the class limit, by upping the bore and stroke to 57·8 × 47·2 mm. On a 13:1 compres-

sion ratio, the watercooled engine produced 46 bhp at 11,500 rpm, but although this was impressive, the other reason for the bike's excellent performance was a dry weight of just 216 lb. Stopping was provided by a massive four-leading shoe Fontana front brake, which was carried in substantial 35 mm Ceriani racing forks.

Following its launch in Italy, the roadster 250TS got off to a slow start in Moto Guzzi's export markets. None at all were imported into the USA, and only a few reached Britain before the appointment in May 1975 of Coburn & Hughes as the marque's new concessionaires. Following the deal with Coburn & Hughes, larger numbers were sold in Britain, at a launch price of £579. This later went up to £599 before the model stopped being imported to Britain in mid-1976. This was on the grounds of what were, in Coburn & Hughes' opinion, excessive numbers of warranty claims associated with the machines, mainly

Milan Show 1975: this customized 250TS cafe racer carried the MotoBi logo. By then MotoBi were part of the same group as Benelli and Moto Guzzi

concerning failures of the left-hand big-end and a poor quality of finish. Strangely the former was probably caused by a batch of faulty bearings, as replacements by the British company Alpha, eliminated the problem.

At the time, I was a Guzzi dealer—and although I had already sold the original Benelli 2C, I found the 250TS much easier to sell, and in general a better-finished motorcycle. But its chrome-work—especially the wheel rims, headlamp brackets and indicator stems—was certainly not up to the rigours of the British weather. All these parts rusted beyond recovery very quickly if not cleaned regularly and protected at the first sign of winter.

It was a shame that details like these, and the poor electrics, detracted from the appeal of a good-looking, fast, sweet-handling bike which bought its rider the exclusivity of the Moto Guzzi name for not much more than the price of a Japanese bike of similar capacity. The 250TS was most certainly not dropped from the British importers' range for anything other than superficial reasons that could easily have been put right had the factory chosen to do so.

Most rides on the standard 250TS ended happily, and one which did so more than most was

Seen at the 1985 IoM TT, a Yamaha RD400 powered 250TS. Its constructor had created an attractive special, with an excellent power to weight ratio

in July 1975 when Fred Sparkes, then chairman of the Barnet and District Motorcycle Club, and his wife Audrey, managed to borrow one of the little Guzzis to replace their defunct Suzuki, on which they had entered for the ACU National Rally. This event, sadly no longer on the calendar, was a great test for the machine and for the rider—the aim being to visit as many checkpoints as possible completing 600 miles in 24 hours on public roads. It also included various special tests at the finishing point, which for that

Half a Benelli/Guzzi '254' four cylinder 250, the 125 four stroke 2C 4T was sophisticated but lacked a competitive price to compete against the Japanese in overseas markets

year's 30th Rally was at Skegness in Lincolnshire. In foul conditions of almost unending rain, the little 250 carried the two passengers and their equipment, including a large tank bag, faultlessly for the whole 24 hours. Fred Sparkes summed up the TS as 'a really good little bike'.

The Milan Show at the end of 1975 saw two developments of the 250TS. The first of these were the updating of the original model to produce the Series 2—a largely cosmetic treatment which made no changes to the engine, frame, or most of the cycle parts. The most significant of the alterations were to the front end, which now received a disc brake, stronger forks and a redesigned instrument console. The 260 mm diameter cast-iron disc was made by Brembo,

with the hydraulic caliper mounted in front of the left-hand fork leg. The forks themselves were of the Guzzi/Benelli group's own manufacture, and were in every way a miniature version of the forks fitted to the V-twin range. In particular, they used the same system of sealed internal damper units. On the top yoke, replacing the previous separate instrument cups, the series 2 had an oblong plastic casing housing both instruments, with a strip of warning lights down the centre. However, the opportunity was not taken to correct one of the minor niggles of the earlier models by relocating the ignition switch, which remained in the same inconvenient position under the front right-hand side of the petrol tank. More significantly, nothing was done about the

major annoyances of the 250TS, its feeble 6-volt electrics and inconvenient petroil mixing.

Milan's other version of the 231 cc two-stroke twin looked much more radically different—a customized, cafe racer styling exercise dressed in a one-piece fibreglass tank and seat moulding, plus a two part full fairing of which the top section turned with the clip-on handlebars, while the lower part with built-in belly pan was fixed. A pair of fashionable cast-alloy wheels and rear-set footrests completed a very full sporting specification. Sadly, this concept remained a non-starter for Moto Guzzi, although a few were produced under the MotoBi name (another famous name that came with Benelli upon De Tomaso's takeover).

Little had been done to the two-stroke twin on take-over, and these two efforts were to be the sum total of all the development work that

Bike for a *pappagallo*? **Flash Jacopo—Jacob's coat of many colours**

was done on it under the Moto Guzzi aegis. Although the model continued to appear at successive shows like the bi-annual Milan exhibition, it soldiered on long after it should have done without radical modernization. It was finally taken out of production in 1982, when it was still recognizable as the badge-engineered Benelli of some eight years before, even down to still being marketed in its original colour scheme!

Some of this lack of attention to the 250TS may have been because Moto Guzzi had another small capacity twin on which to concentrate. This machine, a four-stroke, in theory at least offered Guzzi something rather special in the lightweight field. The 125 2C 4T was in effect one half of the 254, the Benelli/Guzzi four-cylinder 250 which had been launched amid great publicity for the De Tomaso empire at the 1975 Milan Show. For once, De Tomaso had allowed Benelli number one spot and so it was Pesaro, not Mandello, which made the most progress with the miniature four-cylindered show-stealer. With the 250 given to the Benelli camp, Guzzi had to make the most of their half of it.

The 125 2C 4T had an actual capacity of 123·57 cc, using the 254's (actual capacity 231·1 cc) original stroke of 38 mm, but with the bore increased to 45·5 mm. With a single overhead cam driven by a chain between the two barrels, conventional two-valves per cylinder as

Sohc, six-speed 123·57 cc engine, obviously Japanese inspired. Note deep sump and screw-on oil filter

Hard to believe from this shot that it's a 'humble' 125. Actually a nicer bike than one might think

on the four, and a pair of Dell'Orto PHBG 20B carburettors, the little twin produced 16 hp at 10,600 rpm and a five-speed gearbox helped to keep the tiny unit on the boil.

The technology on which the 125 engine was based had a long pedigree. The 254 itself drew upon Guzzi's own 350/400GTS four-cylinder designs of the mid-1970s. But it was even more closely related to Benelli's 500, the 504, which was itself inspired by (some would say, copied from) Honda's sohc four-cylinder engine.

The 125 also made extensive use of the 254's cycle parts, which in themselves used many stock items from the range. These included Guzzi/Benelli forks, a 260 mm Brembo disc front brake and hydraulic system, Sebac rear suspension units, and many proprietary electrical components. In keeping with the more modern approach adopted throughout the design, the electrics were 12-volt, with the improvement that this could be expected to bring to the lighting, ignition and other systems. This was just as well, for starting was exclusively by the button—

no kickstarter was provided.

With an upmarket specification went a stylish trim—silver, with light and dark blue lines on the tank, side panels and seat. All this gave the 125 2C 4T a right to claim equality with any other roadster 125 on the world's markets, except for one thing—price. Its tag automatically excluded potential buyers of utility machines, and those who could afford that bit more unfortunately wanted that bit more, in the form of ccs. Ultimately, this was to determine the model's ability to play a useful part in Moto Guzzi's line-up in the 1980s. Only in the home market, protected from the Japanese competition in the lightweight battlefield by self-imposed tariff barriers, could the diminutive Guzzi be sold in any numbers. While the 254 was similarly highly-priced, its four-cylinder uniqueness ensured it a place of its own in world markets. The 125 2C 4T was just too close to cheaper, well-tried and well-known Japanese designs like the Honda CB125 twin to stand any chance in a purely commercial comparison.

10 | Endurance and record breaking

With much of Guzzi's legendary reputation of the past firmly established in speed events, it was hardly surprising that at the end of the 1960s the Mandello del Lario factory should once again turn its attention to this area. 1957 had marked a dramatic end to Moto Guzzi's participation in tarmac sport, along with fellow Italian marques Gilera and FB Mondial, and at the same time, it seemed as if the final curtain had fallen on what many would still argue was the golden era of Grand Prix road racing. It was virtually inconceivable that Guzzi should so abruptly give up something which they had done so well, but it was a fact—and it took 12 years before Guzzi returned to serious participation in the sport.

This time, when the new 'works' Guzzis appeared in 1969, it was at first solely an attempt at getting the marque's name back in the record books, rather than a full-scale return to the racing circuits. But full racing effort or not, Guzzi was not a factory to do things half-heartedly, and the V-twins machines which they turned out for their record breaking attempt were highly interesting machines in their own right.

Anyone studying the original 700 V7 would have to be excused for failing to notice even a spark of competitive spirit in the make-up of the 90 degree V-twin machine. But Lino Tonti saw something else behind the skin of what most people viewed as simply an out-and-out tourer. Tonti, recently appointed by Guzzi as chief designer to succeed that man of legends and creator of the immortal Guzzi V8 500 GP racer, Giulio Cesare Carcano, realized the importance of proving that Guzzi could still make successful road-racing type machinery.

This was not to decry the fine achievements made by the factory in off-road sport. In the years since Guzzi's withdrawal from Grand Prix competition, they had switched their efforts to this arena, where the highlight was without doubt the 1963 International Six Day Trial held in Czechoslovakia—where both the Italian national teams in the Silver Vase and Trophy contests were 100 per cent Guzzi-mounted. These bikes were singles, not twins, but just how good they were can be judged from the results. All ten starters gained gold medals, and they also took the Silver Vase and three manufacturers' team prizes. Even more amazing was the fact that all the machines were based on current production models—five 125 Stornellos, two 175 and three 250 cc Lodolas.

But with such an illustrious past to live up to, Guzzi found that even the most outstanding results gained in ISDT type events were not enough to satisfy what the press and public wanted—and in fact demanded—of such a famous name. Lino Tonti was acutely aware of this. In addition, he was a thoroughbred road racing enthusiast with his interest and knowledge firmly rooted on the tarmac and with little interest for off-road activities.

With only the unlikely-looking V7 as a basis, he went to work. During the winter of 1968/69, the competition shop at Mandello began the construction of a batch of specially-prepared V7s, stripped of everything that could possibly be removed, in a massive weight saving exercise.

1969 was the year that Guzzi returned to tarmac competition, albeit for world speed record attempts at Monza

This resulted in a machine weighing only 158 kg in which the only standard parts left were the basic engine and gearbox assembly, frame, swinging arm, wheels and front forks. To these were added a handbeaten 29-litre alloy fuel tank, single racing seat, clip-ons and rearsets, plus a final drive box with modified ratios.

Each of the machines was carefully assembled, and their engines were painstakingly tuned. The completed bikes were equipped with full alloy dolphin fairings, made up in three pieces—and, recalling the pukka factory racers of the past, a finish of very pale green paint was applied to the fairing, tank and rear mudguard (no front mudguard was fitted).

The V7 record attempt machines were in fact made in two capacities. Although these were only of marginal difference, they gave Guzzi potential entries in two entirely separate classes. The first engine, for the 750 class, was 739·3 cc, with a bore and stroke of 82 × 70 mm. The other engine was for the 1000 category and used the dimensions of the V7 Special introduced in 1969—757·486 cc, with a bore and stroke of 83 × 70 mm.

The result of these modifications was a full-blooded 68 bhp at the rear wheel at 6500 rpm—an exceptional figure for what had started life very much as a 'cooking' engine—and a large 100 mm white-faced Veglia tachometer kept the pilot informed of how many revs he was extracting.

With the bikes ready to go, the next stage was to select suitable riders. The eight who were chosen turned out to be a good blend of experienced testers and road racers, including such

Part of the 1969 record breaking team, this time with the sidecar attached

well-known names as Remo Venturi, Vittorio Brambilla and Alberto Pagani, while the press were represented by racing journalist Roberto Patrignani. In June 1969, the team was ready to pay its first visit to the famous Monza autodrome on the outskirts of Milan.

Almost at once, it became apparent that the factory had done their homework. What had formerly been very much the ponderous, essen-

Left **Remo Venturi, formally a Grand Prix star with Bianchi, was one of a team of riders. Here he flashes past the Monza pits flat on the tank**

Below **One of the record breaking V-twins without its streamlining in the Monza pit lane. Not such a wild transformation from the standard V7**

tially touring V7 had suddenly taken on a new athleticism and far greater turn of speed. Soon, team members had the deep-sounding V-twins thundering around the track with an enthusiasm that was shortly to be repaid when their leader, Brambilla, set very respectable new 750 cc class records in three categories—the 1000 kilometre at 125·6 mph, 100 kilometres at 131·9 mph, and finally the hour at 132·9 mph.

During October that year, Guzzi returned to Monza to take more solo records, and also went for honours in the sidecar class. In the solo section, the six-hour speed record fell at 125·76 mph, while the twelve-hour went at an average of 111·53 mph. The three-wheel speeds were obviously less, but the one- and six-hour records were both successfully challenged with 115·64 and 86·99 mph respectively.

Besides the considerable amount of healthy publicity that these records generated, Guzzi's efforts also acted as a stepping stone towards the factory making a comeback in the regular road racing arena. But this time, their interest was to be directed not towards the highly-specialized Grand Prix classes, but production racing.

It was here that development of the new 748·4 cc V7 Sport was instrumental in Guzzi's return to competitive tarmac racing, once again at the scene of their recent record-breaking success—Monza. The event was the 500 km endurance race held in June 1971, in which works rider Raimondo Riva headed the Guzzi effort, and for the next two years, Riva, backed up by Ernesto and Vittorio Brambilla, with new-

Unidentified rider on the Monza banking. This photograph gives a vivid impression of the Monza speedbowl section

comers Carena and Gazzola, took the factory-backed V-twins through a string of endurance racing events.

Although never quite as successful as their Bologna rivals, Ducati, Moto Guzzi took many worthwhile placings in races throughout 1972 and 1973. And perhaps more importantly, their entries enabled the factory to develop and test ideas which would otherwise have been difficult, if not impossible, without the spur of competition.

Just one such example was in the same Barcelona 24 Hours race which in 1973 saw one of Ducati's most famous victories with the prototype 860 V-twin. Guzzi themselves had an equally significant entry for the twists and turns of the Montjuich Park circuit—like the Ducati, in the 'prototype' category. This was a machine based on the 750 V7S, but with its engine enlarged to 844 cc, like the then current GT850.

Unlike the production Guzzi 850, however, the new machine was a pure sportster—and it was here, at Barcelona, that the Le Mans, one of the most famous and popular Guzzis of recent times, appeared in embryonic form.

Raimondo Riva and Luciano Gazzola put up a spirited effort aboard the prototype 850 which stayed the full course to finish 5th overall. Grau and Canellas on the winning Ducati had created

Below **Vittorio Brambilla on the Guzzi Sidecar. During the second visit to Monza in October 1969 the one- and six-hour world records were both successfully broken with speeds of 115·64 and 86·99 mph respectively**

Below right **Guzzi and sidecar naked**

Right **V7 powered sidecar sandracer, rider/owner/builder M. Mager of Norway**

history with a record number of 720 laps and Guzzi had put a very creditable performance with their 683 laps completed.

It was therefore not only sad, but surprising, when just two years later in 1975, the factory all but withdrew completely from any form of direct participation in the sport for the second

time. Thereafter, it was left mainly to private race entrants and tuners to carry the Guzzi flag further. One such effort was in June, when the British Royal Air Force team consisting of John Goodall and the late Dave Featherstone finished 5th in the Isle of Man Production TT on a 750S3. One month later, a semi-official 850 Guzzi endurance entry at Mugello came in second, ridden by the team of Sciaresa and Romeri.

1976 started off well for the privateers, with a good result at Daytona, USA. In the production race, Mike Baldwin on expatriate Reno Leoni's brand new 850 Le Mans scored an impressive fifth behind fourth place man Wes Cooley

1970 American racing effort. Ridden by AFM Production class champion George Kerker, this bike was built by ZDS Motor Corporation from a standard touring V7; included in its specification were Rickman front forks and disc front brake. Engine tuning gave a reputed 145 mph

(Kawasaki), Cook Neilson (Ducati), and second and first placed BMWs of Reg Pridmore and winner Steve McLaughlin.

The year also marked the factory's own renewed interest, with a return to the '24 Horas de Montjuic' at Barcelona in early July on a 1000 (948) cc semi-works Guzzi ridden by the old team of Riva and Gazzola who took 9th place with 701 laps completed. This compared favourably with the eventual winners, Stan Woods and Charlie Williams, who covered 741 laps (1755·45 miles) on their works Honda at an average of 73·27 mph.

Later that year, in mid-September, Gazzola and a new partner A. Rusconi finished in 15th position at the French Bol d'Or 24 Hour race. Meanwhile, Riva, now partnered by D. Levieux, came home one place further down the field, in 16th spot.

1977 started exactly like the previous year, with Mike Baldwin recording another fifth place on Reno Leoni's 850 Le Mans at Daytona during the production race in March (now called the

A very wet Bol d'Or 24-hour race was held 11/12 September 1971. Rider here is Vittorio Brambilla

Superbike Production). This time, however, the event was won by Cook Nielson on his 750SS-based Ducati—now with a capacity of 883 cc. Then came a pair of 1000 cc Kawasaki fours, followed by California resident, Briton Reg Pridmore, on a 980 BMW. Baldwin, in fact, had what was reported at the time as the best dice of the day when he caught up with the BMW rider and thereafter a close struggle ensued—victory eventually going to Pridmore by the narrowest of margins.

In the 1977 FIM Coupe d'Endurance series, the

highest Guzzi finishers in any of the rounds were the 12th placing of the Spanish pair A. Perez Rubio/C. Morante on an 850 Guzzi at Barcelona, and the 14th at the Bol d'Or by S. Heltal and M. D'Angelo. Old hand Guzzi endurance rider Raimondo Riva was by now Kawasaki-mounted, finished in eighth spot.

At this time, British riders started to become heavily involved with racing Guzzis. One early exponent was Londoner Jim Wells, who shared with Tony Osborne a specially-prepared home-brewed endurance racer featuring a much-modified 750S3 engine housed in a cantilever frame. Wells had to wait for some time before he was actually to see the chequered flag, at the team's 13th place in the Thruxton 500 at the end of September. This followed a series of problems

Superb action shot of the Riva/Carena works 850 Guzzi at the Zolder 24-hour in Holland 19/20 August 1972. Note the carburettor

which cut short their earlier Coupe d'Endurance efforts, including punctures, a broken crankshaft and oil breather difficulties.

Other Britons who campaigned Guzzis successfully during the same season included the Oxford Fairings team of John Goodall and Doug Lunn. The latter used the Guzzi—a race-kitted Le Mans Mk I—in the four lap, 151 mile Isle of Man Formula 1 TT, in which he finished a highly-creditable 14th, averaging 86·99 mph. The Le Mans was completely standard bar a small fairing and the factory race kit, comprising an open exhaust system, 40 mm Dell'Orto carburettors, racing camshaft and a close-ratio straight-cut gear cluster. It also had the linked brake system discarded in favour of conventional hydraulics with a separate master cylinder. This machine

was electronically timed at just over 138 mph.

Without doubt, the most successful British Guzzi rider of 1977 was Manchester rider Roy Armstrong, on a 1976 Le Mans Mk I, who ended the season by winning the final round—and the championship—of the Avon Roadrunner Production series. Interestingly, both Roy and his fellow racer, younger brother Ian, rode almost completely standard machines throughout the series. Only at the end were special high-

The prototype of what turned out to be the 850 Le Mans was ridden by Riva/Gazzola to fifth spot in the 1973 Barcelona 24 hours. This shot shows Luciano Gazzola aboard. Note Lockheed front brake

Liège 24-hour race, Belgium in 1974. Ferocious action in the Guzzi camp

compression pistons a B10 camshaft, race valve springs, lightened and polished valve gear and modified exhaust added—the winning bike retained its original 36 mm carburettors right through. On this machine, again, the linked brake ystem was converted to conventional hydraulics. Contrary to reports at the time, both Armstrong bikes had been bought and paid for by the brothers, although Roy worked for Manchester-based Sports Motorcycles—Roy can still remember the hire purchase company's name!

Sports Motorcycles did have another connection with track Guzzis, for their director John Sear was also Le Mans mounted. His machine, however, was heavily modified with barrels from a V1000, high compression pistons, race kit cam,

close-ratio gears, and 40 mm Dell'Ortos. With the race kit open exhaust system, this bike was tested by *Motorcycle* at 132·01 mph, but the tester had to sit up for half the length of the strip to keep the revs down in top gear. The standing quarter was covered in 11·8 seconds with a terminal speed of 112·24 mph. Sports Motorcycles were also supplied with a factory-prepared engine unit together with a consignment of special racing spares, but unfortunately, importers Coburn & Hughes held this back for most of the season. . . .

It is little known that the factory 'officially' took part in the 1977 TT. Two works engines were shipped over with factory mechanic Bruno Scola, and were fitted into the chassis of Roy Armstrong and John Sears' Le Mans Mark Is. They were ridden in the Formula 1 event by Steve Tonkin and George Fogarty, but although both had proved

extremely quick in a straight line during practice, unfortunately they were both forced to retire in terrible race conditions, due to sticking carburettor slides on their 40 mm Dell'Ortos.

Both power units had all the factory race kit options, plus a 950 conversion, 47·5 mm inlet and 39 mm exhaust valves, and sintered metal clutch plates. In addition, the machines were fitted with higher-ratio V1000 rear drive bevel gears (with 9/34 teeth) giving a ratio of 1 : 3·788, and because of this, it was also necessary to fit the V1000 universal joint with long rear extension, and V1000 connecting tube to join this with the rear bevel box.

Roy Armstrong cranks his Le Mans around Snetterton's curves on his way to winning the final race, and the championship, in the 1977 Avon Production Bike race series

If the TT had not been a success for the factory, they were secretly delighted with the results of the Avon championship. Not only had Roy Armstrong's Guzzi won, but in addition John Sears was third and Richard Gamble claimed fourth on yet another Le Mans—again with a 950 conversion. Sadly, the following year was to be far less successful for Guzzi enthusiasts in Britain.

Above left **Belle Vue 1977, a Sport Motorcycles of Manchester prepared Le Mans raced by company director John Sear**

Below left **A specially prepared home brewed endurance racer constructed by Londoner Tim Wells, featuring a much modified 750S3 engine housed in a cantilever frame. Co-rider was Tony Osborne during 1977**

Above **Bol d'Or 1982. The fastest Guzzi was this example ridden by Micheli/Gambini/Tamburini. Even though it lost 2¼ hours in the night stemming an oil leak, it still finished in 36th position**

This was because new rules in the Avon Series forced competitors to retain the original capacity of their engine—so putting the Guzzi at an obvious disadvantage. The 844 cc Le Mans engine now had to give away around 150 cc to machines like the Laverda Jota (981 cc) and the increasingly successful and numerous Japanese fours, such as the recently-introduced Suzuki GS1000 (998 cc).

Even in the FIM European endurance championship series, things were getting tougher for the Guzzi V-twin—not helped by the direct participation for the first time of works teams from Honda and Kawasaki. Of the European makes, only Ducati and to a lesser extent, BMW, were able to compete with any hope of success. The only worthwhile results gained by Guzzi in the whole 1978 series were an eighth at Misano in Italy by A. Rusconi/G. Pretto, and a tenth by the Belgian team of M. Biver/E. Guchet at their home event—the first of the six rounds staged.

Despite the popularity of the endurance races, which attract large crowds throughout continental Europe—particularly in France, where there are are now two annual 24 Hour events (at Le Mans in spring and the Bol d'Or in autumn)—the position remains much the same today. But every year sees Guzzi entries—witness, for example, the 1982 Bol d'Or where four Guzzis using racing versions of the Le Mans III engine finished successfully, although the highest only made 17th spot. The fastest of the Mandello V-twins was number 75, ridden by Micheli/Gumbi/Tamburini who had also been quickest of the Guzzis throughout practice. Unfortunately, the team lost $2\frac{1}{4}$ hours during the night in repairing an oil leak, but still finished 34th.

1983 saw the introduction of the Battle of the Twins series into Britain, but the Guzzi V-twin surprisingly never seemed to find the favour with entrants in these events that the other Italian V, the Ducati, did on both sides of the Atlantic. BOTT started in the USA, but even there, John Tesauro on his Le Mans, and California rider Frank Mazur on the ex-Reno Leoni/Mike Baldwin 1970s Superbike production class contender were two of the few North American riders to campaign Guzzis.

The Battle of the Twins came to life for Guzzi in 1984, at no less an event than the March 9th Daytona Heavyweight Modified class, where race history was made when a woman, Sherry Frindus from Gainesville, Florida, scored a surprise win—the first such in an AMA Professional road race, and on a Guzzi, too.

In Britain, the first Guzzi to appear in a Battle of the Twins race was the superbly-prepared Le Mans ridden by its builder and owner, Richard Gamble—the very same who had finished in the 1977 Avon series. He had been persuaded back to the tracks after his retirement, simply for the Twins series, and his red and white showpiece featured many of the engine and cycle parts from his earlier machine. In his first race for five years, he was a comfortable eleventh on a very crisp sounding bike.

Also in 1984, the first Guzzi 90-degree V-twin appeared on the classic racing scene at the British Classic Racing Motorcycle Club's annual Classic race of the year at Snetterton in August. This was ridden by Mark Wellings, who regularly managed to place his 750S3-based racer in the first ten in each of his class races. Such an assured home in classic racing forms a fitting tribute to one of the classic Italian machines of the last two decades.

11 | *Polizia e militaria*

In common with several of the most long-lived and well-established motorcycle manufacturers, such as BMW, Harley-Davidson and Triumph, Moto Guzzi have maintained strong connections with both the police and military authorities over much of the firm's history. This is in no small way a reflection of the type of machines that all four factories have produced—practical, hardwearing and simple in design, offering both a length of service and ease of maintenance not always found in other marques which are either too sporting, over-complicated, or just plain fragile.

The first Guzzi to serve with either the civil or military authorities was the tipo GT17—a development of the civilian GT and GT16 models of 1928 to 1934. Like its civilian counterparts, the GT17, which was built from 1932 until 1939 for military use, was an ohv horizontal single employing the classic Guzzi format of an 88 × 82 mm bore and stroke, giving a capacity of 498·73 cc. Also like the civilian machines, it was fitted with a very early form of spring frame suspension system. Besides service in Italy, the GT17 was used in some numbers in the Italian African colonies, which at that time included Libya and much of East Africa. Several versions were constructed, one of which even mounted a Fiat or Breda light machine gun.

The GT17 was superseded briefly by the similar GT20, before production commenced, in 1939, of the motorcycle which most Italians went to war on—the Alce (elk). This motorcycle was a development of both the earlier military designs,

Above right **Guzzi have a long history of involvement with the military and police authorities; typical example is this 1944 Trialce 500 with drive to both rear wheels**

Below right **The V7 was first conceived mainly with military and police sales in mind. This is an early police production model, year 1967**

Left **Fully kitted police model, with fairing, radio, panniers and sirens**

Right **Italy's presidency guard, the** *Corazzieri,* **pictured in early 1969. In modern times the motorcycle has replaced the horse for many of their escort duties**

and was built in large numbers during the war years in both solo and three-wheel (Trialce) form. Just about every conceivable variation was tried, even including one with skis fitted for mountain patrol work.

Development continued even after hostilities had ceased, and in 1946 an improved version, the Superalce, went into production. This machine remained in service until 1957, but after 1950 it was already starting to be replaced by the Falcone Militare—the service version of the civilian 500 cc Falcone model. From the mid-1950s, this was produced for police use as well, as was the near-identical 250 version, the Airone.

As recounted in chapter 1, the background to the whole V-twin range was the 3 × 3 three-wheel military tractor project, from which sprang the first 90-degree V-twin motorcycle, the V7. Although the V7 was ultimately destined to be a big civilian success, it was itself originally conceived as a police and military motorcycle—to replace the now-aging Falcone singles.

By 1963, both the military and police authorities in Italy had realized that with traffic becoming ever denser and faster, their two-wheeled transport had to be brought into line with the changing conditions. With similar requirements in both fields of duty, it was felt necessary for the two authorities to co-operate in the design and funding of a new motorcycle.

Far from the job of putting a suitable machine together simply being a matter of asking Guzzi to design a replacement for the old faithful Falcone, almost the entire Italian industry was asked to tender for the contract. Designs which were considered (from 1964 to 1967) included submissions from Benelli, Ducati, Gilera—and, of course, Guzzi.

The Benelli, Ducati and Gilera offerings were all parallel twins. Benelli's pushrod twin was eventually to be sold in the late 1960s and early 1970s as the 650 Tornado, while Gilera's effort was an ohc 483·02 cc twin with oversquare 71 × 61 mm bore and stroke, five-speed gearbox and electric start. Although it was well-made, it suffered from a lack of performance compared with the other contenders, with the result that a half-hearted attempt was made to convert it into civilian guise. Its first appearance, in new colours, but still sporting a single seat and radio carrier (less radio) was at the 1967 Milan Show. The Ducati was perhaps the most serious challenger to the V7, but suffered from a distinct lack of funding for a crucial part of its development—and as a result, the first prototype was not constructed until 1967, the same year that the early V7s entered service. Although its dohc 700 cc engine was reputed to be extremely powerful for

and military testers were expressing their full satisfaction with the basic design—the details of which appear in chapter 2. And during December 1964, the first reports of a new machine which had been given the title V7, for V-twin 700 cc, were released to the Italian motorcycle press.

That the V7 was to spawn such exciting sportsters as the V7 Sport, 750S and Le Mans is all the more remarkable when one recalls what a leading Italian journalist, Carlo Perelli, said in March 1965, 'A civilian version of the V7 will follow as soon as expedient. But it should be remembered that this machine has been designed with police and service use in mind—and not just in Italy—and that it is not intended to have any scintillating sporting characteristics'.

The first models of the V7 were supplied to the Italian police in the spring of 1967, at a cost of some 725,000 lire each. The original 703 cc machines were soon to prove both successful and popular with the police patrolman and military despatch rider, whose only criticism was that the bikes lacked power.

This did not deter police forces outside Italy, who had also placed orders for the V7. Amongst these was a rather unusual one from Holland. The Dutch Guzzis were equipped with a single seat sidecar, and the combinations proved so popular that when, in 1969, the larger 757 cc version was announced, there was a repeat order. Even more interesting was a trial purchase of ten V7s (in 757 cc form) from the USA for the Los Angeles Police Department. These were delivered in March 1969, followed soon after by another order for a batch of 85, and many more once the 850 appeared in 1972.

All three engine sizes of the original V7 were used by the Italian police, split into the three divisions of the *Polizia Stradale* (traffic police), *Polizia Urbana* (city police) and *Carabinieri* (local police).

Italian police bikes were usually finished in either military drab green and white, or dark blue and white, although later machines sometimes

its capacity, the Guzzi design was proclaimed the victor, both on its own merits and the factory's ability to come up with the goods within the stipulated time scale.

The original V7 design was the work of Ing. Giulio Carcano, who by then was in the twilight of an outstanding career, and it was soon taken up by his successor, Ing. Lino Tonti, formerly employed by Aermacchi, Bianchi and Gilera. He had also designed the Linto 500 racing twin, basically a pair of 250 Aermacchi Ala d'Oro (golden wings) heads on a common crankcase. And finally, he had assisted Giuseppe Patoni with his exquisite 250, 350 and 500 Paton parallel twin GP racers, a venture part-financed by Bill Hannah, a Scot with business interests in Liverpool.

The first serious studies for the V7 design were commenced in late 1963, and by early 1964, a working prototype had appeared, of what was by now being treated as a priority project by Guzzi, for the Italian motorcycle industry was in decline. Later in the same year, both the police

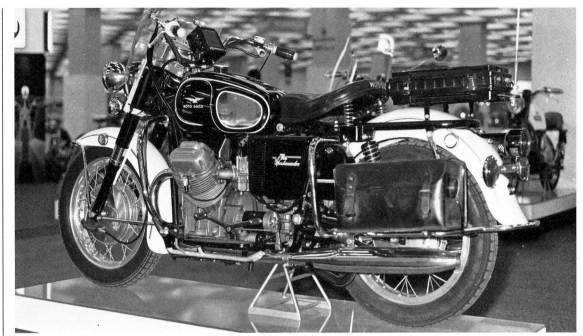

appeared in black and white. For military use, the machine is normally finished in an overall dark green, with only the exhausts and a few minor parts in black.

The introduction in 1975 of the 850T3 meant that even more Guzzi V-twins were sold to both the police and military services throughout the world. By now, several VIP escorts were Guzzi-mounted, in a duty which had formerly been the exclusive domain of Harley, BMW or Triumph. And among the large numbers of overseas buyers which Guzzi later built up, a noteworthy customer was President Fidel Castro of Cuba, on whose orders a fleet of 1000G5 models was supplied in 1982 for use as VIP escorts.

By the late 1970s, virtually every Guzzi V-twin model had been made and sold in either police or military specification, including the V7 700, the V7 750 Special, V7 Ambassador, 850GT, 850 Eldorado, 850T3, T3 California, 1000G5, and even the V1000 automatic. This last bike had been delivered to customers with such diverse requirements as the Sudan State Police in East Africa, and the Municipal Police Department in Louisiana, USA. From the appearance of the very first production V35 and V50s in 1978, police versions of both models were offered. These proved popular because they were inexpensive and suitable for general police duties. By the end of the decade, Guzzi police (and, to a lesser extent, military) motorcycles were in service in every con-

Left **Police 750 Ambassador at the Cologne Show in 1970**

Below left **V1000 I-Convert—'converted' many police forces around the world to automation sooner than expected**

Below **British police Guzzi—the 850T Pursuit, operated by the Norfolk and Sussex Constabulary**

Left **Cuban police operate the V1000G5, which includes VIP escort duty**

Right **Italian police V50, cheap to buy and operate**

V50 'Nato' military bike—perhaps a future role for the Guzzi V-twin lies here, even its survival?

tinent except Australasia.

In Britain, I had supervised the construction and supply of the very first police Moto Guzzi. This, a converted 'civilian' 850T3 California, was supplied to the Norfolk police in 1977, and I well remember delivering the first bike to Kings Lynn police station myself. That the Norfolk police were well satisfied was confirmed when they took the decision to replace their fleet with special, factory-built versions of the police-specification California. Later the larger Sussex force also equipped with 850 Guzzis, now named the Pursuit.

Latterly, Guzzi seem to have realized even more the potential which their wide range of V-twins offered—and convinced partly by the decline in civilian markets for motorcycles worldwide, took the bold decision that for 1985, the factory would catalogue and build four models purely for the police and military markets. These were the 948 cc California Polizia, the 844 cc 850 Carabinieri, and the 490 cc V50s Polizia and Nato.

The California Polizia was the closest to a stan-

dard production model—as the name suggests, the California II. In fact, except for additional blue lights and sirens, it appeared completely stock. The Carabinieri was clearly a much more specialized bike. Not only was the T3, on which it was based, no longer in production, but it had many individual fitments, including a handlebar fairing, special instrumentation, a single saddle, radio and carrier, legshields, front and rear crashbars, panniers, and sirens.

It will be interesting to see how Guzzi shapes up to an obviously serious attempt to secure even more police and military business. I feel that this could well prove the key to just how well Moto Guzzi will fare in the extremely competitive motorcycle sales arena of the last half of the 1980s. Currently, it would appear that their main challenger is BMW, but if Guzzi can finally get their marketing act together, then the sight of a police Guzzi on the motorway, or the Guzzi-mounted soldier escorting a convoy, could become much more the common lot of the V-twins with the eagle emblem. Indeed, the whole future of that famous name may rest upon it.

12 | De Tomaso—power and politics

Alejandro De Tomaso (right) looks pleased to receive an award at a luncheon. A powerful force in both the Italian car and motorcycle manufacturing scenarios

Alejandro De Tomaso was born in Argentina in 1928 into one of the country's most influential families. His father, a leading politician, had died when the young Alejandro was fifteen years old—leaving him, in theory, the most likely successor to the family's large estate near Buenos Aires. However, De Tomaso had other ideas. He saw his future not in the land, but in politics, and his great love, car racing.

Ultimately, the pull of the car world was to prove the stronger. De Tomaso began his racing career in 1951, and he quickly progressed to become one of his native country's top drivers (if a relatively unsuccessful one) in international events—following the pattern of Fangio and Gonzalez, although without their distinguished record. In the early days, he drove privately-entered Maserati sports racing cars, and in March 1956 one of these was entered by De Tomaso and Elizabeth Haskell, an American, for the Sebring 12 Hours in Florida, but retired shortly after the start with gearbox problems.

The next year, De Tomaso decided to leave Argentina and settle in Italy. There were several reasons for this decision—not least of which was that De Tomaso's anti-Peronist activities had led to an unhealthy situation at home. Italy was a logical choice for several reasons. Both sides of his family ancestry had Italian blood, and his love of motor sport also must have suggested Italy as a logical future home.

In 1957, De Tomaso switched his loyalties from Maserati to the Osca factory, founded by the

Maserati brothers, and became factory driver. The team of Haskell and De Tomaso was back together again almost at once, and a highlight of their efforts came on 20 January 1957, when their Osca won its class and finished sixth overall at Buenos Aires. The partnership was soon to become even more close, for on 9 March, Alejandro (who had left his previous marriage the year before) married Elizabeth Haskell in the USA, after which she took the Spanish form of her name and became known as Isabelle De Tomaso.

Following their marriage, the husband and wife team competed together throughout 1957/ 58, while De Tomaso himself continued driving in sports car events with various different partners until 1960. For the first two years, the cars were Oscas, but in 1959, drawing on his wealth, as well as some of Isabelle's considerable fortune, De Tomaso realized a personal dream when be began construction of his own cars in Modena.

At first, De Tomaso's cars were built purely for racing, but by 1963, he had decided that his future lay with the manufacture of production sports cars—albeit for a rather specialist and limited market. The first of these was a handsome Ghia designed coupé called the Vallelunga, which had a four-cylinder Ford engine and was made from 1963–65. This was quickly followed in 1964 by the first of many V8-powered cars, and although these were designed purely for racing, they did form an important part of the De Tomaso jigsaw puzzle.

By 1967, De Tomaso had become properly established, but still only as a small, specialist car builder. But it was this year which was to mark his first serious step up the entrepreneurial ladder towards the top. On De Tomaso's advice, a larger American group, the Rowan Controller Corporation, purchased the well-respected Ghia coachbuilding firm of Turin for some US$650,000. Significantly, Rowan's president was De Tomaso's wife's brother-in-law, and its chairman Amory Haskell was Isabelle's brother. . . . Rowan was

also involved in Alejandro's car construction firm, De Tomaso Automobili.

In 1969, De Tomaso had started on another path which was ultimately to lead him to the door of no less than the Ford Motor Corporation, and proved his ability, even at the highest level, to convince others of their need to participate in a particular project. The result of his discussions was that in 1970, Rowan sold their interests in both De Tomaso Automobili of Modena and Ghia of Turin to Ford—with De Tomaso now as chairman of both companies, and still holding all his share capital in the two organizations. Cleverly, early in 1972, he then sold all these shares to Ford, for a reputed US$2·4 million for De Tomaso Automobili, and around US$5 million for Ghia—making a cool total of almost US$7·5 million!

It was about now that the car constructor and entrepreneur's involvement with motorcycles began to take shape, for with the money he received from the Ford Motor Company, De Tomaso was in a position to take advantage of some investigation work which he had been carrying out over the preceding months into the activities of the ailing Benelli company.

Benelli, based at Pesaro on the Adriatic coast south of Rimini, was once a great name with an exciting past, including success in racing. But by 1971, they had fallen on hard times. With little obvious promise for the company's future, De Tomaso succeeded in acquiring the Benelli plant for a very small sum. And he was shortly to take over a much bigger name, Moto Guzzi, in a joint venture with the Italian government. This was in December 1972, so that within only a very short period of time, one man had effectively gained control of a major slice of the Italian motorcycle industry.

The new combine, called Seimm Moto Guzzi, effectively began trading in early 1973. Right from the start, the two marques involved, Benelli and Guzzi, were to become part of this corporate body, despite their respective factories being over 300 miles apart. But within the group, each was still to retain its own identity and charismatic appeal.

When De Tomaso took them over, Benelli had a very mixed bag of models. These consisted of several mini-bikes, powered by 50 or 65 cc engines and aimed mainly at the American leisure market, a couple of 250 cc ohv singles based on a Motobi design of the early 1960s, and the 650 Tornado parallel twin, which although a soundly-engineered product, was never a very strong seller. Quickly, De Tomaso instigated a whole new range. At the smaller end of the scale, these were two-strokes of 50 cc, 125 cc and 250 cc (the last being a twin)—but much more interesting were the larger bikes, the four-stroke 500 Quattro and 750 Sei.

Both of these multis were clearly based on Honda's design for the CB500/4. The Quattro was almost a direct copy, even down to using Phillips head screws on the engine casings, while the 750 Sei was again very much the same engine, but with two more cylinders. Without a doubt, if De Tomaso had not chosen to pirate Japanese technology, there was no way that Benelli could have launched a six-cylinder 'superbike' a few short months after its total reorganization. As it was, when the 750 Sei appeared in 1973, it caused a sensation, even though its huge amount of publicity was never to be reflected in any real sales success.

De Tomaso's attitude towards the Japanese seems to have been extremely ambivalent, for he expressed a violent opposition to them and to their motorcycle industry but at the same time, he paid them the compliment of Benelli not only producing these two models, but following them with a 250 cc four and even a prototype of a 125 six! All of these models were unmistakably Japanese in inspiration and detail.

Moto Guzzi was able to retain much more of its own identity than Benelli did under De Tomaso, at least in the early years after the take-over. At first, the only outward signs of a clear link between Guzzi and Benelli were when the Benelli two-stroke twins were sold under the Moto Guzzi name. These were followed by the 350/400GTS four-cylinder models sold between 1974 and 1979, and finally by the Moto Guzzi 254, which was of course the much-publicized Benelli 250 Quattro that first appeared at the 1975 Milan Show.

The factor which really managed (successfully) to retain Guzzi's separate identity and the aura of the name, was the V-twin design. This was continued and developed under De Tomaso's auspices, and I am convinced that without the V-twins, Guzzi would never have been able to progress as well as they did in the mid and late 1970s.

An interesting insight into Alejandro De Tomaso (and his wife) came at a meeting which I had with them over dinner in early 1976 at the Canalgrande Hotel in Modena (owned, incidentally, by De Tomaso). The purpose of the meeting was to discuss various business ideas with the British importers, Coburn & Hughes, which could lead to an improvement in British sales.

The aspect I remember most from this two hour meeting was the strong personalities of both the De Tomasos, and in particular, De Tomaso's strong views on his dislike of the Japanese motorcycle industry and his clear approval of involving politicians with his business ideas. It was at this meeting that he suggested a possible discussion between himself and Harold Wilson (then the British Prime Minister) with a view to arranging a link, or at least co-operation, with the Triumph Meriden workers' co-operative. He also voiced his strong distaste for NVT and its board of directors who had dismissed him when an earlier approach had been made to arrange a meeting about a similar co-operative agreement between the Italian (De Tomaso) and British motorcycle industries in an attempt to limit the Japanese expansion into Europe.

Despite such strong ambitions, the only concrete achievement to come from our meeting was the single batch of five hundred Guzzi (Bene-lli) 125 Turismo five-speed two-stroke singles which were shipped to Britain by Moto Guzzi as kits of parts. These were assembled at Meriden and sold in Britain as the 125 Co-uno Moto Meriden. Even this cannot be adjudged a success, because well over 50 of the kits were never assembled by Meriden, but passed to my company, Mick Walker Motorcycles, for the sum of £3500 in September 1978. Of these, around 30 were built up from the kits and sold for a price of £299, while the remainder were broken down to provide a stock of spare parts.

So what led up to this dismal end for what promised to be an interesting period of Anglo-Italian co-operation? After the original meeting with De Tomaso, another discussion was arranged upon our arrival back in England. This was reported in *Motorcycle* 17 April 1976 with the heading 'Moto Meriden bikes start rolling soon'. *Motorcycle* went on to say that 'as revealed last week, Co-operative (Triumph) chairman Denis Johnson met Signor Alessandro

De Tomaso, chief of the Benelli and Moto Guzzi companies in Modena, Italy, last week to finalize the deal whereby he would buy 2,000 machines in kit form and assemble them here'.

Denis Johnson was reported as saying, 'It's all agreed, we're purchasing an initial batch of 2,000 125 cc single-cylinder Moto Guzzis, and hopefully the first crates will arrive by the end of next month, subject to the availability of parts. We'll be painting and distributing the bikes, and Coburn & Hughes will supply marketing, advertising and field sales assistance'.

Later that year, at the Earls Court Show in August, the Co-uno 125 was shown on the Coburn & Hughes stand alongside their Guzzi and Ducati ranges. Dealers were signed up, and Mick Walker Motorcycles had received and binned the initial stock of spare parts. Everyone—distributor, dealer and customer—was ready.

The 125 Moto Meriden Co-uno; an intended bright star that turned out to be very much of a damp squib

What finally happened is a telling example of perhaps the major reason why the Triumph Co-operative finally closed. From August until the following March, not a single 125 Co-uno appeared in a dealer's showroom. When one considers that the kits supplied by Moto Guzzi included a complete engine assembly, and wheels made up with tyres and tubes already on, the construction job which they posed could not have been more straightforward—and one can only wonder why it took Meriden nine months to produce the first bikes. After such a time, both the dealers and the potential customers had almost forgotten about them. Needless to say, after this first debacle, there were no more overtures from De Tomaso to the Triumph Co-operative. . . .

Meanwhile, back in Italy, De Tomaso had bigger things on his plate. For it was also in 1976 that he added Maserati to his growing list of interests. The once-great Italian prestige car firm then joined with another new acquisition, Innocenti, Benelli and Guzzi as part of the De Tomaso group of companies.

Maserati was to have little bearing on De Tomaso's motorcycle interests, but now, Innocenti was to play a major part in the story of the Guzzi twins—for it was this plant which, in 1979, became the home for the mass production of the smaller V-twins, the V35/50, and later the V65.

The Milan facilities, once the home of the Lambretta scooter during the boom days of the 1950s and early 1960s, had then switched to building British BMC cars under licence. These included the best-selling Mini, the Mini Cooper, the earlier A40 and the second series Austin Healey Sprite, and their own Mini-engined 'mini' car. In 1973, the company's founder, Ferdinando Innocenti, died. By this time, the firm had already been swallowed up by the British Leyland group, the successors of BMC, but when Leyland hit financial difficulties, one of the first sections to feel the pinch was Innocenti, with the result that the whole plant and name was sold off to a partnership consisting of De Tomaso and the Italian government body GEPI.

Once again, De Tomaso performed one of his skilful manipulations, for, a matter of months after transferring the entire V35/50 production from Mandello del Lario to the Innocenti plant in Milan, De Tomaso's Seimm Moto Guzzi parent company was able to purchase from the Italian government 76·7 per cent of the Nuova Innocenti share holding. As a result, Innocenti, now widely held to be the most profitable area of De Tomaso's involvement, was placed firmly in the hands of *Il Supremo*.

With so many prominent parts of the Italian car and motorcycle industry under his control, and his avowed hatred of the Japanese, it was perhaps natural that De Tomaso should bring his power to bear on his business partner, the Italian government, in a policy of protection against the invaders, as he saw them—the Japanese Big Four: Honda, Suzuki, Yamaha and Kawasaki. The result was that on 26 May 1977, the Italian government imposed a complete ban on the imports of all Japanese motorcycles. But this bureaucratic decision was plainly read by all well-informed observers of Italian politics as De Tomaso's work, and not that of the nameless officials who rubber-stamped the document.

Of course, the Japanese manufacturers could hardly be expected to take this lying down, and brought pressure on their own government. The result was a protest in which the whole matter was taken to the European Court in Luxembourg for alleged infringement of Common Market regulations. Eventually, for 1978, the import quota for Japanese bikes was raised from nil to 18,000, although it was stipulated that there should be no bikes under 400 cc. This was not much of a victory for Japan, but a good deal better than in 1977.

With hindsight, now that the import of Japanese motorcycles into Italy has become a flood, it could be argued that the Italian authorities did not ultimately help the home producers at all, because in November 1977, they upped VAT to 35 per cent on bikes of over 350 cc, while setting it at 14 per cent for those under 350 cc. At the same time, they imposed a speed limit of 130 km/h (81 mph) on all bikes over 150 cc, and 80 km/h (50 mph) on smaller machines. If anyone gained, it was probably De Tomaso, because of the vast amount of publicity both inside and outside Italy that the issue of the import ban raised in the world's press.

Although the problem of the limited production facilities at Guzzi's Mandello del Lario plant had been solved, there still remained a major difficulty—the need for a central spare parts stockholding strategy. When I visited Guzzi in 1978, major problems could already clearly be seen, and in fact everyone realized this. Not only were the difficulties of storage acute—the stores were in fact a series of small rooms, making it a much more time-consuming exercise to organize, and therefore less profitable than a spares division should have been—but Benelli were suffering similar problems, which were exacerbated by the distance between the two factories.

Even in 1978, senior stores management thought that the simple way to solve the problem would be to have a central parts facility for both factories. And exactly this became a reality when, in 1983, a vast parts complex was opened in Freto, near Modena. This was called the Centro Ricambi (parts centre). One reason for the gap of over five years was that of the stringent Italian labour laws, a complex and time-consuming subject, which held up a quick move because in Italy workers' rights take precedence over a company's desire to move its operations to a more profitable location.

Of all the factories controlled by De Tomaso, the Guzzi plant on the shores of Lake Como a few kilometres north of Lecco is set in the most pleasant surroundings and has one of the most closely-knit of communities. It is therefore hardly surprising that the majority of the workforce, despite relying on Guzzi for a job, hardly wanted to uproot and move to a far less attractive setting in a suburban area.

These moves bring the story of De Tomaso's business (and the Guzzi twins) virtually up-to-date. But what of today and the future?

Up until now, De Tomaso's success has rested firmly on other peoples' failures. Even the Ford Motor Company have to be included in this list, for after paying a great deal of money for De Tomaso Automobili in 1972, they put the company into liquidation in 1975 with the loss of a reported 400 jobs. As for De Tomaso, he played this card to perfection, since even though he 'sold out' to Ford, he has retained his car manufacturing rights and name—still producing De Tomaso automobiles to this day!

At the time of writing, Alejandro De Tomaso effectively controls Guzzi, Benelli, MotoBi, Innocenti, Maserati, De Tomaso cars, and a number of other, smaller companies with such diverse interests as boat building and hotels. It is interesting to note that his earlier declared hatred of the Japanese seems to have mellowed over the years. To illustrate this, he recently concluded a deal with the Japanese car firm of Daihatsu, to supply Innocenti with engines for their minicar—whether this means that he now accepts the Japanese, or just that he will make use of them when in need is an open question.

How does this place the motorcycle part of De Tomaso's corporate body, now that there is a world recession in motorcycle sales? His record to date has been impressive, his rise, breathtaking. But could it be that this very success will eventually prove to be his downfall, with the factories which he now controls suffering the same problems of under-capacity and over-manning which proved their previous owners' downfall? Or will the man display his undoubted talent to its fullest—the talent of being in the best place at the best time for the best deal? Only time will be the judge. . . .

Appendix

1 Specifications

Model	V7 700	V7 Special	V7 Ambassador	V7 Sport
Year	1967–76	1969–71	1969–70	1972–74
Bore (mm)	80	83	83	82·5
Stroke (mm)	70	70	70	70
Capacity (cc)	703·718	757·487	757·487	748·388
Compression ratio (to 1)	9	9	9	9·8
Valve type	ohv	ohv	ohv	ohv
bhp 1	40	45	45	52
@ rpm	5800	6000	6000	6300
Starting system	electric	electric	electric	electric
Oil system	wet sump	wet sump	wet sump	wet sump
Valve timing :	ohv	ohv	ohv	ohv
Inlet opens BTDC	24	24	24	40
Inlet closes ABDC	58	58	58	70
Transfer Exhaust opens BBDC	58	58	58	63
Exhaust closes ATDC	22	22	22	29
Tappets, inlet (mm)	0·15	0·15	0·15	0·22
Tappets, exhaust (mm)	0·25	0·25	0·25	0·22
Primary drive gearing	1·375	1·375	1·375	1·235
Final drive gearing	4·625	4·375	4·375	4·375
Box gearing : 5th				0·750
Box gearing : 4th	0·750	0·750	0·750	0·869
Box gearing : 3rd	0·954	0·954	0·954	1·047
Box gearing : 2nd	1·333	1·333	1·333	1·388
Box gearing : 1st	2·230	2·230	2·230	2·000
No. gears	4	4	4	5
Front tyre	4·00 × 18	4·00 × 18	4·00 × 18	3·25 × 18
Rear tyre	4·00 × 18	4·00 × 18	4·00 × 18	3·50 × 18
Front brake (mm)	drum 220 2LS	drum 220 2LS	drum 220 2LS	d/drum 220 2LS
Rear brake (mm)	drum 220	drum 220	drum 220	drum 220 2LS
Front suspension	teles	teles	teles	teles
Rear suspension	s/arm	s/arm	s/arm	s/arm
Ignition system	coil	coil	coil	coil
Wheelbase (mm)	1445	1470	1470	1470
Ground clear. (mm)	150	150	150	160
Width (mm)	795	830	830	700
Length (mm)	2230	2245	2245	2165
Dry weight (kg)	234	228	228	206

1 bhp figures at rear wheel unless quoted.

Model	750S	750S3	GT850	GT850 California
Year	**1974–75**	**1975–76**	**1972–74**	**1972–74**
Bore (mm)	82·5	82·5	83	83
Stroke (mm)	70	70	78	78
Capacity (cc)	748·388	748·388	844·057	844·057
Compression ratio (to 1)	9·8	9·8	9·2	9·2
Valve type	ohv	ohv	ohv	ohv
bhp	53	53	51	51
@ rpm	6300	6300	6000	6000
Starting system	electric	electric	electric	electric
Oil system	wet sump	wet sump	wet sump	wet sump
Valve timing:	ohv	ohv	ohv	ohv
Inlet opens BTDC	40	20	24	24
Inlet closes ABDC	70	52	58	58
Transfer Exhaust opens BBDC	63	52	58	58
Exhaust closes ATDC	29	20	22	22
Tappets, inlet (mm)	0·22	0·22	0·15	0·15
Tappets, exhaust (mm)	0·22	0·22	0·25	0·25
Primary drive gearing	1·235	1·235	1·235	1·235
Final drive gearing	4·375	4·714	4·714	4·714
Box gearing: 5th	0·750	0·750	0·750	0·7500
Box gearing: 4th	0·869	0·869	0·869	0·869
Box gearing: 3rd	1·047	1·047	1·047	1·047
Box gearing: 2nd	1·388	1·388	1·388	1·388
Box gearing: 1st	2·000	2·000	2·000	2·000
No. gears	5	5	5	5
Front tyre	3·25 H18	3·25 H18	4·00 × 18	4·00 × 18
Rear tyre	3·50 H18	3·50 H18	4·00 × 18	4·00 × 18
Front brake (mm)	d/disc 300	d/disc 300	d/drum 220 2LS	d/drum 220 2LS
Rear brake (mm)	drum 220 2LS	disc 242	drum 220	drum 220
Front suspension	teles	teles	teles	teles
Rear suspension	s/arm	s/arm	s/arm	s/arm
Ignition system	coil	coil	coil	coil
Wheelbase (mm)	1470	1470	1470	1470
Ground clear. (mm)	160	160	150	150
Width (mm)	700	700	830	930
Length (mm)	2165	2165	2245	2245
Dry weight (kg)	206	208	235	255

Model	GT850 Eldorado	850T	850T3	850T3 California
Year	**1972–74**	**1974–75**	**1975–82**	**1975–80**
Bore (mm)	83	83	83	83
Stroke (mm)	78	78	78	78
Capacity (cc)	844·057	844·057	844·057	844·057
Compression ratio (to 1)	9·2	9·5	9·5	9·5
Valve type	ohv	ohv	ohv	ohv

bhp	51	53	53	53
@ rpm	6000	6000	6000	6000
Starting system	electric	electric	electric	electric
Oil system	wet sump	wet sump	wet sump	wet sump
Valve timing:	ohv	ohv	ohv	ohv
Inlet opens BTDC	24	20	20	20
Inlet closes ABDC	58	52	52	52
Transfer Exhaust opens BBDC	58	52	52	52
Exhaust closes ATDC	22	20	20	20
Tappets, inlet (mm)	0·15	0·22	0·22	0·22
Tappets, exhaust (mm)	0·25	0·22	0·22	0·22
Primary drive gearing	1·235	1·235	1·235	1·235
Final drive gearing	4·714	4·714	4·714	4·714
Box gearing: 5th	0·750	0·750	0·750	0·750
Box gearing: 4th	0·869	0·869	0·869	0·869
Box gearing: 3rd	1·047	1·047	1·047	1·047
Box gearing: 2nd	1·388	1·388	1·388	1·388
Box gearing: 1st	2·000	2·000	2·000	2·000
No. gears	5	5	5	5
Front tyre	4·00 × 18	3·50 H18	3·50 H18	3·50 H18
Rear tyre	4·00 × 18	4·10 H18	4·10 H18	4·10 H18
Front brake (mm)	d/drum 220 2LS	disc 300	d/disc 300	d/disc 300
Rear brake (mm)	drum 220	drum 220	disc 242	disc 242
Front suspension	teles	teles	teles	teles
Rear suspension	s/arm	s/arm	s/arm	s/arm
Ignition system	coil	coil	coil	coil
Wheelbase (mm)	1470	1470	1470	1470
Ground clear. (mm)	150	160	160	150
Width (mm)	830	780	780	960
Length (mm)	2245	2200	2200	2200
Dry weight (kg)	235	202	205	225

Model	**850T4**	**850T5**	**850 Le Mans**	**850 Le Mans II**
Year	**1980–83**	**1983–85**	**1976–78**	**1978–80**
Bore (mm)	83	83	83	83
Stroke (mm)	78	78	78	78
Capacity (cc)	844·057	844·057	844·057	844·057
Compression ratio (to 1)	9·5	9·5	10·2	10·2
Valve type	ohv	ohv	ohv	ohv
bhp	55·94	55·94	71 1	71 1
@ rpm	6750	6750	7300	7300
torque (Kg-m)	6·36	6·36	7·8	7·8
@ rpm	5500	5500	6660	6660
Starting system	electric	electric	electric	electric
Oil system	wet sump	wet sump	wet sump	wet sump
Valve timing:	ohv	ohv	ohv	ohv
Inlet opens BTDC	20	20	20	20

Inlet closes ABDC	52	52	52	52
Transfer Exhaust opens BBDC	52	52	52	52
Exhaust closes ATDC	20	20	20	20
Tappets, inlet (mm)	0·22	0·22	0·22	0·22
Tappets, exhaust (mm)	0·22	0·20	0·22	0·22
Primary drive gearing	1·235	1·235	1·235	1·235
Final drive gearing	4·714	4·714	4·714	4·714
Box gearing: 5th	0·750	0·750	0·750	0·750
Box gearing: 4th	0·869	0·869	0·869	0·869
Box gearing: 3rd	1·047	1·047	1·047	1·047
Box gearing: 2nd	1·388	1·388	1·388	1·388
Box gearing: 1st	2·000	2·000	2·000	2·000
No. gears	5	5	5	5
Front tyre	3·50 H18	110/90 H16	3·50 X18	100/90 X18
Rear tyre	4·10 H18	130/90 H16 **2**	4·00 × 18	110/90 H18
Front brake (mm)	d/disc 300	d/disc 270	d/disc 300	d/disc 300
Rear brake (mm)	disc 242	disc 270	disc 242	disc 242
Front suspension	teles	teles	teles	teles
Rear suspension	s/arm	s/arm	s/arm	s/arm
Ignition system	coil	coil	coil	coil
Wheelbase (mm)	1470	1505	1470	1470
Ground clear. (mm)	160	140 **3**	175	175
Width (mm)	780	760	720	720
Length (mm)	2200	2150	2190	2190
Dry weight (kg)	211	220	198	202

1 crankshaft rating   **2** 130/90 H18 from mid-1984   **3** 150 from mid-1984

Model	850 Le Mans III	1000 Le Mans	V1000 I-Convert	1000SP
Year	1981–84	1984–85	1975–84	1978–80
Bore (mm)	83	88	88	88
Stroke (mm)	78	78	78	78
Capacity (cc)	844·057	948·813	948·813	948·813
Compression ratio (to 1)	9·8	10	9·2	9·2
Valve type	ohv	ohv	ohv	ohv
bhp	76 **1**		50 **2**	54·91
@ rpm	7700		6250	6250
torque (Kg-m)	7·6	8·43		8·6
@ rpm	6200	6250		5200
Starting system	electric	electric	electric	electric
Oil system	wet sump	wet sump	wet sump	wet sump
Valve timing:	ohv	ohv	ohv	ohv
Inlet opens BTDC	20	32	20	20
Inlet closes ABDC	52	57	52	52
Transfer Exhaust opens BBDC	52	65	52	52
Exhaust closes ATDC	20	27	20	20
Tappets, inlet (mm)	0·22	0·20	0·22	0·22
Tappets, exhaust (mm)	0·22	0·20	0·22	0·22

Primary drive gearing	1·235	1·235	1·570	1·235
Final drive gearing	4·714	4·714	3·788	4·714
Box gearing: 5th	0·750	0·750		0·750
Box gearing: 4th	0·869	0·869		0·869
Box gearing: 3rd	1·047	1·047		1·047
Box gearing: 2nd	1·388	1·388	1·333	1·388
Box gearing: 1st	2·000	2·000	1·100	2·000
No. gears	5	5	2	5
Front tyre	100/90 V18	120/80 V16	100/90 H18	100/90 H18
Rear tyre	110/90 V18	130/80 V18	110/90 H18	110/90 H18
Front brake (mm)	d/disc 300	d/disc 270	d/disc 300	d/disc 300
Rear brake (mm)	disc 242	disc 270	disc 242	disc 242
Front suspension	teles	teles	teles	teles
Rear suspension	s/arm	s/arm	s/arm	s/arm
Ignition system	coil	coil	coil	coil
Wheelbase (mm)	1505	1500	1470	1480
Ground clear. (mm)	175	175	150	160
Width (mm)	640	640	850	750
Length (mm)	2190	2180	2200	2180
Dry weight (kg)	206	215	229	210

1 crankshaft rating   **2** approx. figure due to convertor losses

Model	**1000SP NT**	**V1000G5**	**1000 California II**	**250TS drum**
Year	**1984–85**	**1978–83**	**1981–85**	**1974–75**
Bore (mm)	88	88	88	56
Stroke (mm)	78	78	78	47
Capacity (cc)	948·813	948·813	948·813	231·523
Compression ratio (to 1)	9·2	9·2	9·2	9·75
Valve type	ohv	ohv	ohv	ts
bhp	54·91	54·91	58·12	24·5
@ rpm	6250	6250	6750	7570
torque (Kg-m)	6·88	6·88	7·7	
@ rpm	3000	3000	5200	
Starting system	electric	electric	electric	kick
Oil system	wet sump	wet sump	wet sump	Petrol/oil mix
Valve timing:	ohv	ohv	ohv	
Inlet opens BTDC	20	20	20	
Inlet closes ABDC	52	52	52	
Transfer Exhaust opens BBDC	52	52	52	
Exhaust closes ATDC	20	20	20	
Tappets, inlet (mm)	0·22	0·22	0·22	
Tappets, exhaust (mm)	0·22	0·22	0·22	
Primary drive gearing	1·235	1·235	1·235	2·944
Final drive gearing	4·714	4·714	4·714	2·411
Box gearing: 5th	0·750	0·750	0·750	0·875
Box gearing: 4th	0·869	0·869	0·869	1·045
Box gearing: 3rd	1·047	1·047	1·047	1·300

Box gearing: 2nd	1·388	1·388	1·388	1·857
Box gearing: 1st	2·000	2·000	2·000	2·833
No. gears	5	5	5	5
Front tyre	100/90 H18	100/90 H18	120/90 H18	3·00 × 18
Rear tyre	110/90 H18	110/90 H18	120/90 H18	3·25 × 18
Front brake (mm)	d/disc 300	d/disc 300	d/disc 300	d/drum 180
Rear brake (mm)	disc 242	disc 242	disc 242	drum 158
Front suspension	teles	teles	teles	teles
Rear suspension	s/arm	s/arm	s/arm	s/arm
Ignition system	coil	coil	coil	electronic
Wheelbase (mm)	1480	1470	1565	1330
Ground clear. (mm)	160	160	155	165
Width (mm)	750	780	890	770
Length (mm)	2180	2200	2370	1970
Dry weight (kg)	210	220	250	132

Model	**250TS disc**	**V35**	**V35II**	**V35C**
Year	**1976–82**	**1977–79**	**1980–85**	**1982–85**
Bore (mm)	56	66	66	66
Stroke (mm)	47	50·6	50·6	50·6
Capacity (cc)	231·523	346·23	346·23	346·23
Compression ratio (to 1)	9·75	10·8	10·8	10·8
Valve type	ts	ohv	ohv	ohv
bhp	24·5	27	29·07	29·07
@ rpm	7570	7750	7750	7750
torque (Kg-m)		2·80	2·80	2·80
@ rpm		6750	6750	6750
Starting system	kick	electric	electric	electric
Oil system	petroil/oil mix	wet sump	wet sump	wet sump
Valve timing:	ts	ohv	ohv	ohv
Inlet opens BTDC		18	18	18
Inlet closes ABDC		50	50	50
Transfer Exhaust opens BBDC		53	53	53
Exhaust closes ATDC		15	15	15
Tappets, inlet (mm)		0·10	0·10	0·10
Tappets, exhaust (mm)		0·15	0·15	0·15
Primary drive gearing	2·944	1·846	1·846	1·846
Final drive gearing	2·411	3·875	3·875	3·875
Box gearing: 5th	0·875	0·909	0·909	0·909
Box gearing: 4th	1·045	1·045	1·045	1·045
Box gearing: 3rd	1·300	1·277	1·277	1·277
Box gearing: 2nd	1·857	1·733	1·733	1·733
Box gearing: 1st	2·833	2·727	2·727	2·727
No. gears	5	5	5	5
Front tyre	3·00 × 18	90/90 × 18	90/90 × 18	100/90 H18
Rear tyre	3·25 × 18	3·00 × 18	3·00 × 18	130/90 H16
Front brake (mm)	disc 260	d/disc 260	d/disc 260	d/disc 260

Rear brake (mm)	drum 158	disc 235	disc 235	disc 235
Front suspension	teles	teles	teles	teles
Rear suspension	s/arm	s/arm	s/arm	s/arm
Ignition system	electronic	electronic	coil	coil
Wheelbase (mm)	1330	1395	1395	1460
Ground clear. (mm)	165	165	165	160
Width (mm)	770	750	750	960
Length (mm)	1970	2080	2080	2080
Dry weight (kg)	132	152	152	164

Model	V35 Imola	V35 Imola II	V50	V50II
Year	1979–83	1984–85	1977–79	1979–80
Bore (mm)	66	66	74	74
Stroke (mm)	50·6	50·6	57	57
Capacity (cc)	346·23	346·23	490·30	490·30
Compression ratio (to 1)	10·5	10·5	10·8	10·8
Valve type	ohv	ohv	ohv	ohv
bhp	27·83	40 1	45 1	45 1
@ rpm	8000	8800	7500	7500
torque (Kg-m)	2·73	2·73	4·08	4·08
@ rpm	6750	6750	5500	5500
Starting system	electric	electric	electric	electric
Oil system	wet sump	wet sump	wet sump	wet sump
Valve timing:	ohv	ohv	ohv	ohv
Inlet opens BTDC	18	18	18	18
Inlet closes ABDC	50	50	50	50
Transfer Exhaust opens BBDC	53	53	53	53
Exhaust closes ATDC	15	15	15	15
Tappets, inlet (mm)	0·10	0·10	0·10	0·10
Tappets, exhaust (mm)	0·15	0·15	0·15	0·15
Primary drive gearing	1·846	1·846	1·642	1·642
Final drive gearing	3·875	3·875	3·875	3·875
Box gearing: 5th	0·909	0·909	0·909	0·909
Box gearing: 4th	1·045	1·045	1·045	1·045
Box gearing: 3rd	1·277	1·277	1·277	1·277
Box gearing: 2nd	1·733	1·733	1·733	1·733
Box gearing: 1st	2·727	2·727	2·727	2·727
No. gears	5	5	5	5
Front tyre	3·25 × 18	100/90 V16	100/90	3·00 × 18
Rear tyre	3·50 × 18	120/90 V16	100/90	3·50 × 18
Front brake (mm)	d/disc 260	d/disc 270	d/disc 260	d/disc 260
Rear brake (mm)	disc 235	disc 235	disc 235	disc 235
Front suspension	teles	teles	teles	teles
Rear suspension	s/arm	s/arm	s/arm	s/arm
Ignition system	coil	coil	electronic	electronic
Wheelbase (mm)	1420	1450	1395	1395
Ground clear. (mm)	165	165	165	165

Width (mm)	700	700	750	750
Length (mm)	2080	2080	2080	2080
Dry weight (kg)	169·5	168	170	170

1 crankshaft rating

Model	**V50III**	**V50C**	**V50 Monza**	**V50 Monza II**
Year	**1980–85**	**1982–85**	**1980–83**	**1984–85**
Bore (mm)	74	74	74	74
Stroke (mm)	57	57	57	57
Capacity (cc)	490·30	490·30	490·30	490·30
Compression ratio (to 1)	10·4	10·4	10·4	10·4
Valve type	ohv	ohv	ohv	ohv
bhp	39·91	39·91	41·07	50 **1**
@ rpm	7500	7500	8000	7800
torque (Kg-m)	4·08	4·08	3·97	
@ rpm	5500	5500	6500	
Starting system	electric	electric	electric	electric
Oil system	wet sump	wet sump	wet sump	wet sump
Valve timing:	ohv	ohv	ohv	ohv
Inlet opens BTDC	18	18	18	18
Inlet closes ABDC	50	50	50	50
Transfer Exhaust opens BBDC	53	53	53	53
Exhaust closes ATDC	15	15	15	15
Tappets, inlet (mm)	0·10	0·10	0·10	0·10
Tappets, exhaust (mm)	0·15	0·15	0·15	0·15
Primary drive gearing	1·642	1·642	1·466	1·466
Final drive gearing	3·875	3·875	3·875	3·875
Box gearing: 5th	0·909	0·909	0·909	0·909
Box gearing: 4th	1·045	1·045	1·045	1·045
Box gearing: 3rd	1·277	1·277	1·277	1·277
Box gearing: 2nd	1·733	1·733	1·733	1·733
Box gearing: 1st	2·727	2·727	2·727	2·727
No. gears	5	5	5	5
Front tyre	3·00 × 18	100/90 H18	100/90 V16	100/90 V16
Rear tyre	3·50 × 18	130/90 H16	120/90 V16	120/90 V16
Front brake (mm)	d/disc 260	d/disc 260	d/disc 260	d/disc 270
Rear brake (mm)	disc 235	disc 235	disc 235	disc 235
Front suspension	teles	teles	teles	teles
Rear suspension	s/arm	s/arm	s/arm	s/arm
Ignition system	coil	coil	coil	coil
Wheelbase (mm)	1395	1460	1420	1450
Ground clear. (mm)	165	160	165	165
Width (mm)	750	960	700	700
Length (mm)	2080	2080	2080	2080
Dry weight (kg)	169	165	169·5	170

1 crankshaft rating

Model	125 2C 4T	V65	V65SP	V65C
Year	1979–83	1981–85	1981–85	1982–85
Bore (mm)	45·5	80	80	80
Stroke (mm)	38	64	64	64
Capacity (cc)	123·57	643·4	643·4	643·4
Compression ratio (to 1)	10·65	10	10	10
Valve type	ohc	ohv	ohv	ohv
bhp	16·3 **1**	52 **1**	52 **1**	52 **1**
@ rpm	11000	7050	7050	7050
torque (Kg-m)		4·51	4·51	4·51
@ rpm		6500	6500	6500
Starting system	electric	electric	electric	electric
Oil system	wet sump	wet sump	wet sump	wet sump
Valve timing:	ohc	ohv	ohv	ohv
Inlet opens BTDC		18	18	18
Inlet closes ABDC		50	50	50
Transfer Exhaust opens BBDC		53	53	53
Exhaust closes ATDC		15	15	15
Tappets, inlet (mm)		0·10	0·10	0·10
Tappets, exhaust (mm)		0·15	0·15	0·15
Primary drive gearing		1·642	1·642	1·642
Final drive gearing		3·875	3·875	3·875
Box gearing: 5th		0·909	0·909	0·909
Box gearing: 4th		1·045	1·045	1·045
Box gearing: 3rd		1·277	1·277	1·277
Box gearing: 2nd		1·733	1·733	1·733
Box gearing: 1st		2·727	2·727	2·727
No. gears	5	5	5	5
Front tyre	2·75 × 18	100/90 H18	100/90 H18	100/90 H18
Rear tyre	3·00 × 18	110/90 H18	100/90 H18	130/90 H16
Front brake (mm)	disc 260	d/disc 260	d/disc 260	d/disc 260
Rear brake (mm)	drum 158	disc 235	disc 235	disc 235
Front suspension	teles	teles	teles	teles
Rear suspension	s/arm	s/arm	s/arm	s/arm
Ignition system	coil	coil	coil	coil
Wheelbase (mm)	1290	1460	1460	1460
Ground clear. (mm)	155	165	165	160
Width (mm)	750	730	730	960
Length (mm)	1870	2200	2200	2200
Dry weight (kg)	110	165	180	166

1 crankshaft rating

Model	V65 Lario	V65TT	V35TT	1000SPII
Year	1984–85	1984–85	1984–85	1984–85
Bore (mm)	80	80	66	88
Stroke (mm)	64	64	50·6	78
Capacity (cc)	643·4	643·4	346·23	948·813

Compression ratio (to 1)	10·3	10	10·5	9·2
Valve type	ohv	ohv	ohv	ohv
bhp	60 **1**	48 **1**	33 **1**	58·12
@ rpm	7800	7400	8300	6750
torque (Kg-m)				6·54
@ rpm				5750
Starting system	electric	electric	electric	electric
Oil system	wet sump	wet sump	wet sump	wet sump
Valve timing:	ohv	ohv	ohv	ohv
Inlet opens BTDC	18	18	18	20
Inlet closes ABDC	50	50	50	52
Transfer Exhaust opens BBDC	53	53	53	52
Exhaust closes ATDC	15	15	15	20
Tappets, inlet (mm)	0·10	0·10	0·10	0·22
Tappets, exhaust (mm)	0·15	0·15	0·15	0·22
Primary drive gearing	1·642	1·642	1·846	1·235
Final drive gearing	3·875	3·875	3·875	4·714
Box gearing: 5th	0·909	0·909	0·909	0·750
Box gearing: 4th	1·045	1·045	1·045	0·869
Box gearing: 3rd	1·277	1·277	1·277	1·047
Box gearing: 2nd	1·733	1·733	1·733	1·388
Box gearing: 1st	2·727	2·727	2 727	2·000
No. gears	5	5	5	5
Front tyre	100/90 V16	3·00 × 21	3·00 × 21	110/90 H16
Rear tyre	120/90 V16	4·00 × 18	4·00 × 18	130/80 H18
Front brake (mm)	d/disc 270	disc 260	disc 260	d/disc 270
Rear brake (mm)	disc 235	disc 260	disc 260	disc 270
Front suspension	teles	teles	teles	teles
Rear suspension	s/arm	s/arm	s/arm	s/arm
Ignition system	coil	coil	coil	coil
Wheelbase (mm)	1450	1490	1490	1505
Ground clear. (mm)	165	168	168	150
Width (mm)	700	880	880	760
Length (mm)	2080	2080	2080	2150
Dry weight (kg)	172	165	160	220

1 crankshaft rating

2 Colours

1967

V7 700

Metallic red tank, with chrome knee recesses, silver mudguards side panels, toolboxes and front fork bottoms. Black frame, swinging arm, fork yokes and spring covers, suspension unit bodies, stands, tail light and support. Pinstriping on tank in white on side panels in red. 'Moto Guzzi' eagle decals on tank, 'V7' on side panels, chrome-plated exhaust system, headlamp rim, bottom front fork spring covers, rear suspension springs, front mudguard stays, handlebars, crashbar, seat grab rail and handlebar lever clamps. Polished alloy wheel rims, foot pedals and instrument console.

1968

V7 700

As above but with all white finish replacing previous red and silver finished items. More comprehensive pinstriping, in red, on mudguards, tank, side panels and toolboxes, '700 cc' added to 'V7' on panels. Black fork bottoms.

V7 Special

As 1968 V7 700, but pinstriping details changed, larger in white. Two thin red stripes above and below. Eagle in red above. New side panels, with grills, V7 Special and black stripe 4 in. below. Arrow emblem in black and red on toolboxes. Alloy instrument console now finished in black.

V7 Ambassador

As V7 Special, but metallic red tank, panels and toolboxes, white pinstriping. Silver mudguards. Side reflectors on both mudguards.

850GT

As V7 Special, but metallic red tank, panels and toolboxes. White lining. No eagle transfers on tank, only Moto Guzzi and two thin lines above and below. '850GT' and V shape logo with two thin lines at each side on side panels, two straight horizontal lines on toolboxes. Chrome-plated mudguards.

850 Eldorado

As GT but with white tank, panels, toolboxes and mudguards. Eagle transfer on tank lining in red. Also some Eldorados in overall black, with white lining including, mudguards. 'Eldorado' on side panels '850' on toolboxes, both with double thin white line.

1971–74

757/850GT California

As GT, but overall black finish with white lining. Black panniers. Two-colour 'buddy' seat, black top, white sides. Eagle transfer on tank.

1971

V7 Sport

Lime metallic green tank, with black horizontal line, with Moto Guzzi in white, one thin line above and below in white. Lime green side panel with V7 Sport transfer. Italian racing red for frame and swinging arm. Black fork yokes, rear light instrument console at centre stand. Silver fork bottoms. Polished alloy alternator cover, rocker covers and wheel rims. Stainless steel mudguards. Chrome mudguard stays, headlamp shell and rim clip-ons, and exhaust system.

1972–73

V7 Sport

As above but with metallic cherry red tank and panels with tank and side panel transfers in white. Black frame and swinging arm. Some V7 Sports were also sold with lime green tank and panels, but black frame and swinging arm.

750S

Overall black finish but with thick and thin stripes in either red, orange or green across the tank and side panels. 'Moto Guzzi' badges on tank with '750S' on side panels. Black silencers otherwise as V7 Sport.

750S3

As 750S, but black headlamp shell chrome crashbar.

850T

Either brown, salmon or metallic green for tank and side panels. Gold metal tape above and below 'Moto Guzzi' metal badge on tank. '850-T' metal badge on side panels. Black frame, swinging arm, stands, fork yokes and instrument console. Polished stainless steel mudguards. Chrome-plated headlamp shell and rim, exhaust system, rear light bracket, headlamp brackets, indicator bodies, seat grab rail, crashbar and mudguard stays. Alloy wheel rims.

850T3

As 850T. But with additional colour options of black, silver or metallic ice blue, with gold or white pinstriping replacing the metal foil tape on 850T. Black headlamp shell, silver painted front fork bottoms. Black rear light support. 850-T3 side panel badges.

850T3 California

As all black 850T3, but with black panniers, with horizontal white lines and 'Moto Guzzi' decal. Tinted screen. Chrome-plated crashbars, pannier supports and rear carrier.

850T4

As T3 except silver painted cast alloy wheels, burgundy tank, panels and fairing, with gold lining.

1984

850T5

Metallic gold/brown tank, side panels, fairing, seat base, front mudguard and front fork bottoms, with red lining, and yellow upper edging. Black frame swinging arm stands, suspension unit bodies upper part of fairing. Matt black for much of instrument console area, rear mudflap and minor parts. Silver cast wheels. Chrome exhaust system, foot pedals and rear suspension springs. Moto Guzzi badges on front sides, above headlight on fairing and above rear light on seat. 850T5 1985 overall silver replaced gold/brown. No striping. Black rocker box covers as 850 Le Mans.

850 Le Mans I

Italian racing red, metallic light grey/blue (also a few in white from March 1977) for tank, mudguards, side panels and fairing. Up to early 1977 a dayglo orange section was on fairing around headlamp. Frame, swinging arm, stands and fork bottom, plus top and bottom areas of tank in matt black as were headlamp bracket, headlamp shell and rim and complete exhaust system. Silver painted cast alloy wheels. Black indicator bodies, black clip-on handlebars and lever chrome suspension unit springs, horn grill and tank cap.

850 Le Mans II

As Le Mans, but red (or royal blue in the UK only) with colour matched fairing with black upper and lower section on top section with black area on fairing side sections around cylinder heads. '850 Le Mans II' side panel badges. Some British bikes finished in black and gold, at the end of production.

850 Le Mans III

As above, but in red, white or metallic grey, no black area on fairing. Main colour on rear of seat and fork bottoms. Black rear mudguard. Chrome exhaust system. Gold 'Moto Guzzi' eagle decals on tank, '850 Le Mans III' badge on side panels. Orange flashes on fairing.

1000 Le Mans

Red or white tank, fairing, side panels, seat, front mudguard wheels, bottom detachable frame tubes, belly pan and fork bottoms. Black frame swinging arm, suspension unit springs, exhaust system, rocker boxes covers and rear mudguard. Dayglo flashes on each side of upper fairing.

1000SP

Metallic gold or silver tank, fairing and fairing side panel, and both mudguards. Black for bottom and bottom areas of tank and fairing side panels in recesses around cylinder heads and top and bottom of tank. Black frame, swinging arm indicators, handlebar controls. Tinted fairing screen, silver wheels and fork bottoms. Chrome suspension springs, grab rail, exhaust system and foot pedals. Also available as the Royale in Britain in metallic cherry red and silver, or with British made Sigma panniers as the Black Prince in all black finish with gold pinstriping and wheels.

1000SP NT

As standard SP, but with either metallic light green or metallic ice blue, no black on top fairing or fuel tank. For 1982/83 red was offered for fairing, tank, panels and mudguards. For the tank, panels and top section of the fairing a contrasting white over half the area was introduced.

1000SPII

As 850T5 1984, but with red fairing with gold/brown relief. Black rocker box covers.

V1000 I-Convert

As 850I3 but with silver, black or metallic ice blue as main colour. Stripes in black for silver or ice blue or either gold or white for black. Rear light cover, panniers and small aerofoils in main colour.

V1000G5

As V1000 Convert, but also in salmon red.

1000 California II

Dark brown or white tank, side panels and centre sections of mudguards. Silver wheels and fork bottoms. Tinted screen, black (natural plastic) panniers. Black frame, swinging arm, stands, headlamp shell. Black and white 'buddy' seat. Chrome exhaust system, crashbars, pannier mounts, rear carrier seat grab rail, handlebars, headlamp rim, indicator bodies outside area of mudguards, mudguards stays, horns, air cleaner cover, rear number plate/light support and foot pedals. Moto Guzzi metal tank badge, California II decals for side panels.

250TS drum

Metallic—lime green, kingfisher blue or golden brown, with gold pinstriping. Tank metal 'Moto Guzzi' badge, side panels metal '250TS' badges. Black frame, swinging arm, chainguard, instrument console. Chrome exhaust system, mudguards, wheel rims, headlamp brackets, headlamp shell and rim, indicators and supports, suspension springs, rear light support, petrol cap and handlebars. Polished alloy fork yokes and bottoms.

250TS disc

As drum brake version, but black fork yokes and silver fork bottoms. Chrome rear grab rail.

V35/50

Italian racing red or metallic blue/grey for tank, side panels, mudguards and headlamp (some of the latter were also finished in chrome or matt black). Black frame, swinging arm, stands, fork yokes, indicators, headlamp shell and rim handlebar control levers and supports, also the top and bottom section of the tank. Silver cast wheels and fork bottoms. Chrome exhaust system, grab rail, rear suspension springs, grab rail and foot pedals. 'Moto Guzzi' tank badge and V35/50 side panel badges in metal. Polished alloy rocker box covers and alternator cover.

V50II

As above but with red/yellow stripes on front and side panels. 'V50II' badges on latter. Chrome-plate headlamp rim, indicators and stems. Unpainted alloy swinging arm. Black plastic alternator cover.

V50III

Main colours now red or brown, otherwise as V50II but black indicators, stems and headlamp brackets. No black on top of tank. Rear light support now integral with rear mudguard and in that colour. The stripes on the tank and panels were changed to ones of deep red and gold.

V35II

As V50II but in red or silver. From 1982 also available in metallic lime green. Black indicators on some models.

V35/50/65C

Red or metallic steel blue/grey for tank and side panels, with the former having black/gold lining, the latter blue/black. Black frame, stands and instrument console and handlebar levers. Chrome exhaust, mudguards, headlamp brackets, suspension springs, grab rail, rear light support, air filter cover, foot pedals. Silver wheels. 'Moto Guzzi' metal badges on tank, 'V35/50/65C' badges on side panels.

V35 Imola/V50 Monza

Red or metallic ice blue tank, fairing, seat tail, side panels, mudguards, with red or black fork bottoms respectively. Black wheels, with polished alloy side rims. Black frame, suspension springs, rear light, handlebars, stands and bottom/top of tank and front of side panels. 'Moto Guzzi' eagle transfers for tank. 'V35 Imola/V50 Monza' transfers for side panels.

V65

As V50III but in red, lime metallic green or steel grey with various colour stripes. Chrome-plated headlamp brackets and colour matched seat tail. Metal tank and side panel badges.

V65SP

As V65, but colour matched fairing.

125 2C 4T

Silver tank, side panels, seat tail, front mudguard, cast wheels and headlamp brackets. Black headlamp shell, instrument console, top and bottom fork yokes, indicators and stems, chainguard, rear mudguard frame, swinging arm and centre stand. Dark and light blue and white flashes for tank, panels and seat tail. Chrome engine side covers, headlamp rim and exhaust system. Moto Guzzi on tank and 125 on side panels transfers.

V35TT and V65TT

White, red or metallic deep grey/gold with red/blue stripes on tank, main colour also on side panels rear tail section, headlamp holder and front mudguard. Red frame, suspension unit bodies, fork bottoms front composition number plate, fork yokes and seats, with 'TT' in blue. Black exhaust system, rocker covers, fork gaiters, rear mudguard, handlebars and levers and front brake hub. 'Guzzi' for tank and V35/V65 for panels, transfers in red.

V35 Imola II, V50 Monza II and V65 Lario

Red, metallic light grey or white in same layout as Le Mans 1000, but with respective side panel badges and silver fork bottoms. On red bikes all frame was in red.

3 Carburettor settings

Model	Year	Dell'Orto type	Size	Main	Pilot	Slide	Needle	Needle position	Needle jet
V7 700	1967	SS1 29D/DS	29	135	55	100	M14	1	265
V7 700	1968–76	VHB 29CD/CS	29	135	45	80	V5	2	265
V7 750 Special	1969–71	VHB 29CD/CS	29	145	45	60	V5	2	265
V7 Ambassador	1969–70	VHB 29CD/CS	29	145	45	60	V5	2	265
V7 Sport	1972–74	VHB 30CD/CS	30	142	50	40	V9	2	265
750S	1974–75	VHB 30CD/CS	30	142	50	40	V9	2	265
750S3	1975–76	VHB 30CD/CS	30	142	50	40	V9	2	265
GT850	1972–74	VHB 29CD/CS	29	145	45	60	V5	2	265
GT850 California	1972–74	VHB 29CD/CS	29	145	45	60	V5	2	265
GT850 Eldorado	1972–74	VHB 29CD/CS	29	145	45	60	V5	2	265
850T	1974–75	VHB 30CD/CS	30	120	50	40	V9	2	265
850T3	1975–82	VHB 30CD/CS	30	120	50	40	V9	2	265
850T3 California	1975–80	VHB 30CD/CS	30	120	50	40	V9	2	265
850T4	1980–83	VHB 30CD/CS	30	120	50	40	V9	2	265
850T5	1983–85	VHBT 30CD/CS	30	130	50	40	V9	2	265
850 Le Mans	1976–78	PHF 36BS/BD	36	140	60	603	K5	2	265AB
850 Le Mans II	1978–80	PHF 36BS/BD	36	140	60	603	K5	2	265AB
850 Le Mans III	1981 84	PHF 36BS/BD	36	115	50	603	K18	3	265AB
1000 Le Mans	1984–85	PHM 40ND/N6	40	145	57	605	K19	3	268AB
V1000 I-Convert	1975–84	VHB 30CD/CS	30	125	50	40	V9	2	265
1000SP	1978–80	VHB 30CD/CS	30	125	50	40	V9	2	265
1000SP NT	1980–83	VHB 30CD/CS	30	125	50	40	V9	2	268
V1000G5	1978–83	VHB 30CD/CS	30	125	50	40	V9	2	265
1000 California II	1981–85	XHB 30CD/CS	30	125	50	40	V9	2	265
250TS drum	1974–75	VHB 25BS/BD	25	98	45	50	E30	2	260S
250TS disc	1976–82	VHB 25BS/BD	25	98	45	50	E30	2	260S
V35	1977–79	VHBZ 24FS/FD	20	102			E	2	260AH
V35II	1980–85	VHB 26FS/FD	26	108	40	40	E26	2	260AH
V35 Imola	1979–83	VHB 26FS/FD	26	108	40	40	E27	2	260AH
V35 Imola II	1984–85	PHBH 28BD/BS	28	115	45	50	X6	2	268T
V50	1977–78	VHBZ 24FS/FD	24	105	40	40	E2	2	260AH
V50II	1979–80	VHBZ 24FS/FD	24	105	40	40	E2	2	260AH
V50III	1980–85	PHBH 28BS/BD	28	118	50	50	X6	3	268T
V50C	1982–85	PHBH 28BS/BD	28	118	50	50	X6	3	268T
V50 Monza	1980–83	PHBH 28BS/BD	28	118	50	50	X6	3	268T
V50 Monza II	1984–85	PHBH 30BS/BD	30	105	40	40	X8	1	268T
125 2C 4T	1979–83	PHBG 20B	20	92	35	30	W2	2	258BP
V65	1981	PHBH 30BS/BD	30	105	40	40	X8	2	268T
V65SP	1981–85	PHBH 30BS/BD	30	105	40	40	X8	2	268T
V65C	1982–85	PHBH 30BS/BD	30	105	40	40	X8	2	268T
V65 Lario	1984–85	PHBH 30BS/BD	30	110	40	40	X8	2	268T
V65TT	1984–85	PHBH 30BS/BD	30	105	40	40	X8	2	268T
V35TT	1984–85	VBH 26FS/FD	26	108	40	40	E26	2	260AH
1000SPII	1984–85	VHB 30BS/BD	30	112	50	503	K27	2	262ABI

4 Prices

May 1972			Importer
V7 Sport	£1350		Rivetts Ltd
850GT	£1145		143 Grosvenor Road
V7 Special	£920		London SW1

November 1974			Importer
250TS	£674		Barretts of Redhill
750S	£1380		Station Approach
850T	£1346		Redhill, Surrey

May 1975			Importer
250TS	£579.50		Coburn & Hughes
850T	£1479.50		21 Park Street
850T3	£1599.50		Luton
850T3 California	£1699.50		Beds.
750S3	£1749.50		

July 1976	
850T	£1479
850T3	£1599
850T3 California	£1699
850 Le Mans	£2000
V1000 Convert	£1899

July 1977	
850T3	£1799
850T3 California	£1999
850 Le Mans	£1999
V1000 I-Convert	£2199

July 1978	
850T3	£1799
850T3 California	£1999
850 Le Mans	£1999
V1000 I-Convert	£2199
1000 Spada	£2399

June 1979	
V50	£1475
850T3	£1999
850T3 California	£2359
850 Le Mans	£2477
1000 Spada	£2299
Spada Royale	£2799

August 1980	
V50	£1489
850T3	£2299
850T3 California	£2499
850 Le Mans II	£2639
1000 Spada NT	£2709

May 1981	
V50	£1499
V50 Monza	£1699
850T4	£2699
850T3 California	£2799
850 Le Mans III	£3199
Spada NT	£2899

February 1982	
V50	£1599
V50 Monza	£1749
850T4	£2479
850T3 California	£2499
California II	£2899
850 Le Mans III	£2899
Spada NT	£2799
Mistral	£3249

August 1983	
V50	£1799
V50 Monza	£1899
850 Le Mans III	£3299
California II	£3399
Spada NT	£3199

February 1984	
V35II	£1999
V50III	£2199
V65	£2299
V65SP	£2399
V65C	£2529
T5 Milano	£3459
850 Le Mans III	£3399
California II	£3599
Spada NT	£3459

April 1985		Importer	V35 Imola	£2699
V35II	£1999	Three Cross Motorcycles	V65 Lario	£2899
V50II	£2199	Woolsbridge Industrial Estate	850TS	£2999
V65	£2399	Three Legged Cross	1000SPII	£3899
V65SP	£2499	Wimborne	California II	£3999
V65TT	£2699	Dorset	1000 Le Mans	£3999
V65C	£2699			

5 Model recognition

These notes are to some extent a precis of the main text and should be used in conjunction with it and the other appendices.

1967

V7 700 went on sale, 703 cc, 90 degree ohv V-twin. 4-speed, r/hand gearchange, shaft drive, one piece crankcase, chrome cylinder bores 4-ring pistons single coil value springs, 29 mm Dell'Orto SS1 carburettors, electric start, belt driven generator, 12-volt. 20-litre fuel tank, 35 mm enclosed fork, 220 mm drum brakes 4·00 × 18 tyres, front crashbars. Threaded exhaust ports (for ex. pipe retention).

1968

V7 700 continued, but with square slide Dell'Orto VHB carburettors, seat with hump at rear.

1969

V7 700 discontinued (except for police/military sales).

  V7 Special introduced 757 cc larger valves, twin valve springs. Sold in USA as Ambassador with sealed beam headlight and side reflectors.

1970

V7 Special/Ambassador continued.

1971

V7 Special/Ambassador continued. **V7 California** introduced. Americanized with western bars, buddy seat, panniers, front and rear crashbar, carrier, windshield, Chrome-plated mudguards.

  V7 Special/Ambassador discontinued late in year.

1972

V7 California continued, but now with 844 cc engine and 5 speeds. **850GT** introduced, based on 757 cc **V7 Special** but with larger engine capacity and 5 speeds. Chrome-plated mudguards and direction indicators. Sold in USA as **Eldorado** with sealed beam and side reflectors.

  V7 Sport introduced, new lower full cradle frame, with detachable bottom rails. Double sided front brake. Swan neck adjustable clip-ons. 22·5-litre sports tank, stainless steel mudguards (rear hinged), chrome-plated exhaust system, with slashed silencer ends. Triangular side panels. 3·25 × 18 front, 3·50 × 18 rear tyre, 748 cc engine 5-speed alternator, 30 mm Dell'Orto VHB carburettor. Exposed fork legs.

1973

GT850/Eldorado, California and **V7 Sport** continued.

1974

V7 Sport continued.

  GT850/Eldorado, California now with Brembo disc front brake and Lucas direction indicators. Left-hand gearchange.

  250TS introduced 2-stroke piston port 231 cc twin, 5-speed, electronic ignition 6-volt, 32 mm Marzocchi forks. Double sided SLS drum front brake 18 in. steel rims, l/hand gearchange.

  Mid year **V7 Sport, GT850/Eldorado** and **California** discontinued.

  750S introduced, based on **V7 Sport** but with timing chain replacing gears in timing cover. Double Brembo disc front brake, new bump stop saddle, matt black silencers.

850T introduced sports/tourer with **V7 Sport** frame and forks. Single disc front brake clamp up exhaust pipes, seamed silencers, finned rear brake plate. 30 mm Dell'Orto VHB carburettors. 170 mm Aprilia headlamp with chrome rim and shell. Square rear light. 3·50 × 18 front 4·00 × 18 rear tyres. Lockable toolboxes. 25-litre fuel tank. Front crashbars, l/hand gearchange, alternator.

1975

250TS, 850T, 750S continued.

Early in year **750S** and **850T** discontinued.

750S3, 850T3 and **850T3 California** introduced. All three with patented linked triple Brembo disc brake system. **750S3** cross between **750S/850T3**, non-adjustable clip-ons, front crashbar, square rear light, Aprilia indicators, **750S** curved exhaust pipes, but with **T/T3** clamped exhaust pipe retention method. Black silencers.

850T3 similar to **T**, but with non-lockable side panels, black headlamp shell, higher handlebars and linked brake system. **T3 California** as **T3**, but with windshield, footboards, western (braced) bars, dual colour 'buddy' saddle, front and rear crashbars, carrier and panniers.

Mid year **V1000 I-Convert** introduced semi automatic 2-speed gearbox, with torque convertor. 948 cc. Cycle parts mixture of **T3** and **T3 California** parts. More luxurious saddle. Electro fuel tap. Safety devices including automatic mechanical caliper on rear disc to enable parking on a gradient.

1976

250TS, 850T3, T3 California, V1000, 750S3 continued.

250TS now with single 260 mm Brembo disc front brake, square instrument console and forks based on V-twins with sealed internal damper units.

Early in year **850 Le Mans** introduced 844 cc engine, 36 mm carburettors. Larger valves, higher compression pistons. Drilled brake discs, flyscreen, plastic mudguards and side panels. Foam rubber hump back saddle, cast alloy wheels.

Mid year **750S3** discontinued.

Late in year **T3 California Rally** introduced, painted mudguards, no tacho, speedo from **V1000**.

1977

250TS, 850T3, T3 California, V1000 and **Le Mans** continued.

Le Mans now with improved saddle and oblong rear light.

Middleweight 90 degree shaft drive V-twins introduced in 350 (**V35**) and 500 (**V50**) form. Identical spec. triple linked disc brakes, cast wheels, front master cylinder mounted at front of tank near steering head. Lockable fuel cap. 24 mm Dell'Orto VHB carburettors. Electronic ignition, two piece crankcases. All black headlamp shell and rim.

Mid year **California Rally** discontinued.

1978

250TS, V35, V50, 850T3, T3 California, V1000 and **Le Mans** continued.

Manual version of **V1000** introduced, **V1000G5** with 5 speeds and clutch from **T3**.

SP (Spada) introduced 3-piece full fairing with tinted screen, clock and voltmeter and additional warning lights. Cast wheels, new saddle, new silencers slightly upswept like **Le Mans**, but in chrome.

Autumn **Le Mans II** introduced, **SP** type fairing and instrumentation. Brake calipers at rear of fork legs.

1979

250TS, 850T3, T3 California, V1000, V1000G5, Le Mans II, 1000SP, V35 and **V50** continued.

850T3 now with cast wheels, CEV headlamp, oblong rear light, **SP** saddle and switchgear. Black plastic alternator cover, locking filler cap, **T3 California** with lock cap, plastic alternator cover, CEV headlamp and improved switchgear. **V1000, G5** similarly modified.

Updated version of **V50, V50II** 2·5 litre sump, plastic alternator cover, chrome-plated headlamp rim, polished fork yokes.

125 2C 4T introduced. Sohc chain driven 4-stroke twin. Dell'Orto PHBG 20 mm carburettors, 5-speed, electric start, 12-volt, cast wheels, disc front brake.

End of year **V35 Imola** sports model introduced. Standard **V35** engine with larger valves. Bikini fairing, clip-ons, rear sets, dual racing seat, upswept silencers.

1980

125 2C 4T, 250TS, 850T3, T3 California V1000, Le Mans II, 1000SP, V35 and **V50II** continued.

Early in year **1000SP NT** introduced, most with Nikasil coated cylinder bores, but all with seamless, more restrictive silencers and **V1000** saddle. **1000SP** discontinued.

850T4 introduced similar to **SP NT**, but with 850 engine, and without fairing side panels.

V35II introduced 26 mm carburettors, brake calipers at rear of fork legs, new saddle, black plastic timing cover, chrome indicators and stems, new silencers, points ignition. **V35** discontinued.

V50 Monza introduced. Same spec as **V35 Imola**, but with **V50III** engine.

V50III introduced larger valves, 28 mm carburettors, points, ignition. Front master cylinder moved to handlebar, drilled brake discs, oblong indicators. One piece indicator stems/headlamp bracket and grill. Plastic front mudguard. **V50II** discontinued, but late ones also with drilled discs.

Le Mans II now with Nickasil coated bores, improved internal fork dampers, air assisted fork operation, Paioli rear suspension units, although specifications do overlap.

Year end **T3 California** and **Le Mans II** discontinued.

1981

125 2C 4T, 250TS, 850T3, 850T4, V1000, V1000G5, SP NT, V35II, Imola, V50III, Monza continued.

850 Le Mans III introduced. Square finned barrels/heads. New silencers, exhaust system chrome-plated. Smaller fairings with new spoiler attached to cylinder heads. Centrally mounted 100 mm white faced Veglia tacho. Front indicator mounted outside fairing. Swinging arm 2 in. longer. 25-litre fuel tank, new tank and seat design new side panels. Cast alloy latticework for footrests/pedal support.

1982

125 2C 4T, 250TS, 850T3, 850T4, V1000, V1000G5, SP NT, V35II Imola, V50III, Monza, Le Mans III continued.

1000 California introduced, **Le Mans III** square head/barrel castings, but with 948 cc capacity. Windshield, western bars, buddy seat, panniers, front and rear crashbars, carrier, cast wheels. **Spada NT** exhaust system. New design for tank, seat, side panels. Chrome-plated deeply valenced mudguards, chrome trim on side covers.

V35C/V50C/V65C introduced. US custom style. Identical specification except engine and carburettor sizes. 15-litre peanut tank, stepped dualseat. **Imola/Monza** silencers. Western bars. Chrome headlamp brackets, rear light brackets and mudguards. Side reflector on direction indicators.

V65 (Normale) introduced larger version of **V50III**, but with new dualseat, chrome headlamp brackets and minor differences, 30 mm carburettors.

V65SP (Special) introduced version of **V65** with **SP** (Spada) type 3-piece fairing.

End of year **250TS** and **850T3** discontinued. (**T3** still available to order for police work.)

1983

125 2C 4T, 850T4, V1000, V1000G5, 1000SP NT, V35II, Imola, V50III, Monza, V35/50/65C, V65, V65SP and **850 Le Mans III** continued.

Mid year **850T4, V1000** and **V1000G5** discontinued. **850T5** introduced, mini fairing (no screen) 16 in. wheels, triple 270 mm discs, twin air horns, square fin barrels/ heads and 22·5-litre tank.

End of year **1000SP, Imola** and **Monza** discontinued.

1984

125 2C 4T, V35II, V50III, V35/50/65C, V65, V65SP, 850 Le Mans III and **850T5** continued.

V35 Imola II, V50 Monza II and **V65 Lario** introduced. 4-valve cylinder heads, **Le Mans III** type fairing and spoilers, including instrument layout and 100 mm centrally mounted white face Veglia tacho. Black exhaust system. 16 in. wheels. Nickasil coated cylinder barrels, clip-ons and belly pan.

V35TT and **V65II** introduced, enduro styled trail bikes, identical except engine and carburettor sizes. Motocross type 14-litre fuel tank, plastic MX type front mudguard, with mudflap. Leading axle 38 mm. Marzocchi front forks, single disc front and rear brake. Braced handlebars, flexibly mounted oblong direction indicators, prop stand only. Akront alloy wheel rims 3·00 × 21 front, 4·00 × 18 rear enduro tyres.

1000 Spada II introduced based on **850T5** but with larger 948 cc engine, **SP** 3-piece fairing and 18 in. rear wheel.

Early in year **T5** updated, 18 in. rear wheel, screen now fitted.

Late in year **850 Le Mans III** discontinued. **1000 Le Mans** introduced, styling similar to **Imola II/Monza II** and **Lario**, black exhaust system 16 in. front, 18 in. rear wheels. 270 mm triple discs, 40 mm carburettors.

End of year **125 2C 4T** discontinued.

1985

V35II, V35 Imola II, V35C, V35TT, V50III, V50 Monza II, V50C, V65, V65SP, V65 Lario, V65C, V65TT, 850T5, 1000SPII, California II and **Le Mans** continued.

Custom models now with special dualseat, with extended grab rail and carrier. Small mudflap at base of front mudguard. **V65C** offered with windshield panniers, front crashbar and hydraulic steering damper.

Following police/military models offered, **V50 Polizia, V50 NATO, 850 Carabinieri** and **California Polizia**.

6   Model chart

V7 700	703	1967–1969	1000 California II	949	1982–1985
V7 750 Special	757	1969–1971	250TS drum	231	1974–1975
V7 Ambassador	757	1969–1971	250TS disc	231	1976–1982
V7 Sport	748	1972–1974	V35	346	1977–1979
750S	748	1974–1975	V35II	346	1980–1985
750S3	748	1975–1976	V35C	346	1982–1985
GT850	844	1972–1974	V35 Imola	346	1979–1983
*GT850 California	844	1972–1974	V35 Imola II	346	1984–1985
GT850 Eldorado	844	1972–1974	V50	490	1977–1979
850T	844	1974–1975	V50II	490	1979–1980
850T3	844	1975–1982	V50III	490	1981–1985
850T3 California	844	1975–1980	V50C	490	1982–1985
850T4	844	1980–1983	V50 Monza	490	1980
850T5	844	1983–1985	V50 Monza II	490	1984–1985
850 Le Mans	844	1976–1978	125 2C 4T	124	1979–1985
850 Le Mans II	844	1978–1980	V65	643	1982–1985
850 Le Mans III	844	1981–1984	V65SP	643	1982–1985
1000 Le Mans	949	1984–1985	V65C	643	1982–1985
V1000 I-Convert	949	1975–1984	V65 Lario	643	1984–1985
1000SP	949	1978–1980	V65TT	643	1984–1985
1000SP NT	949	1980–1983	V35TT	346	1984–1985
V1000G5	949	1978–1983	1000SPII	949	1984–1985

*Also in 757 cc form 1971

These dates are for actual factory production periods, not
when the models were offered for sale, or made their public
debut at shows.